M000169874

The Sky Is NOT the Limit

The Fletcher Cleaves Story

by Fletcher D. Cleaves

Copyright © 2019 Fletcher D. Cleaves

All rights reserved. Except as permitted under the U.S.
Copyright Act of 1976, no part of this publication may be
reproduced, distributed, or transmitted in any form or by
any means, or stored in a database or retrieval system,
without the prior written permission of the publisher.

One11 Publishing
Hendersonville, TN 37075

www.one11publishing.com

Publisher: Sedrik Newbern, Newbern Consulting, LLC
Editor: Linda Wolf, Network Publishing Partners, Inc.
Cover Designer: Joshua Swodeck, Swodeck, Inc.

Printed in the United States of America
First Edition: December 2019

ISBN Paperback: 978-1-7343537-2-3

Library of Congress Control Number: 2019920028

One11 Publishing is an imprint of
Newbern Consulting, LLC.

This book is dedicated to my parents and
my grandmother, and to all my friends and family
who have supported me through this journey.

But most importantly, this book is dedicated to those
who feel that a severe setback is the end of your chances
for happiness! I hope you will see that there is no end
to your chances, because I am continuously doing things
that make me happy and pushing life to the limit!
May you overcome your obstacles and
prove the haters wrong!

Table of Contents

Chapter 1   It Happens

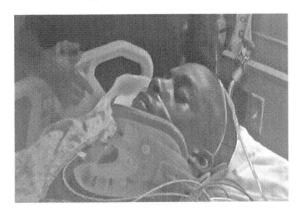

In a flash of blue light, my life was changed forever. It was a beautiful evening after a rainy day in September, and almost kickoff time for the first NFL game of 2009. My roommate Dayne and I were driving back from Buffalo Wild Wings to our dorm to watch the game. I could smell those wings in the back seat waiting for us. We were talking about what first-year college guys talk about—girls, sports, and whether the Titans or the Steelers were going to win. We were football scholarship students at Lambuth University, excitedly gearing up for our first college game.

As I was driving, I checked my rearview mirror when Dayne suddenly yelled, "Fletch, watch out!" I realized that the oncoming car was crossing the double yellow line, coming straight at us. In that moment, I saw the woman who was driving that car. She was looking down, and the blue light of a device lit her face in the growing darkness around us.

I panicked. The 1988 Samurai I had driven in high school did not have power steering, so I had to use some muscle to turn it. But this 1999 Honda Accord had power steering. In my desperation, I didn't have time to think about power steering. I overcorrected and jerked the wheel too hard.

I know she must have been able to see in her rearview mirror the result of her decision to look down at her screen instead of at the road, but she never stopped to see if we were okay. Her car raced away out of sight, but my car was already spinning out of control.

I heard a deafening BOOM! as we hit a guardrail and then the car was airborne. We seemed to be floating weightless over a bridge and toward a steep embankment. It was surreal. Each second stretched out like ripples widening in a pool. I could tell that I was upside down. I remember thinking, 'Man, we are in the air for a long time!'

I braced for impact. After months of intense training for my first year of college football, I felt my body tensing for the toughest tackle of my life. It was like running a ball across the middle of the field when you know you're going to get hit, but you don't know exactly when. I kept expecting it, and I knew it would be bad. Yet even though it couldn't have taken more than a few seconds for us to crash at the bottom of that deep ditch, it was like watching an eerie slow-motion playback moment from a big game.

I remember pulling my head down toward my shoulders in anticipation. But I don't remember the crash itself. I was knocked unconscious immediately. I don't know how long I was out, but when I came around, I noticed that the roof of the car had caved in. The next thing I heard was Dayne's voice yelling, "Fletch! Fletch!" which immediately woke me up. In my mind, I thought he was trying to wake me up in our dorm room and I was just asleep. But it was so dark, and all around us was a misty fog.

My first thought was, 'My dad's going to kill me. I just got this car!' It was my high school graduation gift in June from my parents. I tried to roll over, but I couldn't move. I was pinned under the roof of the car, lying on my right arm. Then I tasted mud and leaves, and I began to realize I was in a serious situation.

Dayne was trying to get me out of the car, but he was so badly injured and bleeding that he couldn't do it. Why wasn't I feeling any pain? Why couldn't I move? Then I had a thought that made my blood run cold. If it started raining again, that ditch could flood, submerging us in brown, muddy water. I couldn't seem to turn my head to see anything out of the window. But out of the corner of my eye, I saw moonlight glinting on a large puddle of water very close to the car.

I tried not to panic, but when Dayne said he was going for help, I begged him, "Please don't leave me here by myself! I don't want to die!"

"Fletch, we gotta get you out of there!" he said. "I promise you, I'm going to make it back." Then he was gone. I couldn't help crying. It was terrifying being down there alone like that, hidden from the road above, as evening darkened around me and the sound of cars going by became less frequent. I wanted to scream for help but for some reason, I didn't have power in my lungs or throat.

It seemed like an eternity being trapped there, unable to move. I thought about my parents and wondered if this was how my life was going to end, stuck in a car at the bottom of a ditch here in Jackson, Tennessee. Other thoughts raced in my head as if my brain was spinning out of control. 'How am I going to get out of here? We've got practice in the morning. Am I going to be able to play football tomorrow? What's wrong with my legs?'

The tears rolled down my face. I calmed myself saying, "C'mon, man. You've been working out all this time—you should be able to muscle your way out of this car. Come on, Fletcher. One, two, three ..."

Nothing.

I figured my legs must be broken, but how could that be if I didn't feel any pain? How could I reach my parents? How badly was I hurt? I thought about my family, then about my friends from high school and my teammates. At last, I heard the sirens of the ambulance, then the voices of the ambulance driver and the paramedics at the edge of the ditch. Someone yelled, "Is anybody down there?"

I thought I was yelling back, "Down here!" but I couldn't raise my voice at all.

Someone else said, "Hey, I see somebody down there. Are you alive?"

I wanted to say, "No, I'm speaking from beyond the grave." And I thought, '*Are you alive?* What kind of question is that?!'

The floodlights from the ambulance were so bright in that dark ditch that I had to squint as I heard people racing toward me. They used the Jaws of Life, a hydraulic tool that pries metal apart to open up cars in emergencies, to get me out. Because I was lying on my right side, they had to pull me out of the car by my left arm. That was the first time I felt pain in my arm and my neck, and I yelled, "Please stop!

Please stop! Something's wrong." They hoisted me up the steep climb in a gurney with some type of crane.

In the back of the ambulance, a young woman examined me. I felt her touching my neck. Then I could hear her going through my pockets, but I couldn't feel a thing. I was thinking, 'Wow, that's weird.'

She asked so many questions. "Where are you? Do you know what happened? What's your name? Can you move your arm?"

"Yes, I was in a car crash. My name is Fletcher Cleaves. I'm 18 years old," I said, trying to steady my voice. I moved my right arm for her.

"Can you move your other arm?"

I moved my left arm.

She said, "I want you to move your right leg." I moved my right leg. Then she paused. She said, "Please move your right leg."

And I said, "I did!"

She paused again. "Okay," she said. "Move your left leg."

I moved my left leg. Another pause. Then she said it again. "Can you move your left leg?"

"I did," I said, feeling confused.

She didn't meet my eye, but I saw her look of concern. "Okay," she said, "we're going to take you to the emergency room for some tests." That's when I knew that something was very wrong. She talked with someone in a low voice, and then she said, "We think you might have broken your neck."

Immediately, I asked to call my parents. Little did I know that the hospital staff had already called them, but because I was older than 18, they could only inform my parents that I was in a car crash and that they should come to the hospital right away. HIPAA privacy laws restricted the staff from providing any more details.

By the time I called them, my parents were frantically driving to Jackson from Memphis. My dad was so relieved to hear me sounding coherent that he didn't seem concerned at all when I told him I broke my neck. At that time, none of us knew exactly what that might mean in terms of recovery and long-term disability.

In the kung fu movies I watched, a guy would break his neck and immediately fall down dead and that was that. So, the fact that I had a broken neck and I was still talking didn't make sense to me. Even though my dad was just as confused, he told me, "Fletcher, when we got the call from the hospital that you had been in a crash, we didn't know what to think. But then when you called us and I heard you making sense and sounding like yourself, I knew that whatever else might be wrong, we can deal with it. We are on our way to you right now."

A cold feeling of dread started in my shoulders and settled on me all the way to the hospital. At the hospital, I learned the truth. The roof of the car had caved in and broken my neck in two places. That was what had knocked me unconscious.

So many people in white coats and scrubs were rushing around me, checking my vital signs, taking blood, and asking questions. My neck was locked in a brace to keep me from moving it, so all I could do was look up at the glare of the ceiling lights and try to stop shaking. I couldn't wait for my parents to arrive. I just wanted to see a familiar face.

I didn't get to see Dayne at the hospital right away, as another team was busy working on him. A doctor in the ER asked me, "Are you sure you and Dayne were in the same car?" He had an incredulous look on his face. "He's all banged up, and you don't have a scratch on you."

He told me that Dayne had been ejected from the car and must have been thrown against a tree or some bushes. His arm had been so badly injured, and he was in such a state of shock, no one could figure out how he managed to climb up a steep eight-foot embankment to get help. Dayne said later that he felt like an angel was pushing him saying, "You have to make it, you have to make it."

A young off-duty police officer had found Dayne stumbling in a church parking lot, covered with blood and disoriented, clutching his arm. The officer called 911, and Dayne tried to tell her, "You have to find my friend. The car crashed. He's trapped down there in the ditch." She couldn't make sense of what he had said because his speech was so slurred, and then he passed out. But the paramedics spotted the car and rushed down to search for me.

I wished I could talk with him about it, but there was too much going on for both of us at that point. When my parents arrived, they comforted me and kept telling me I was going to be okay. They told me that some of my coaches and other players from the team had already arrived and were waiting for news about Dayne and me. The nurse announced that they had to cut my clothes off so that they wouldn't have to move my legs or my neck. I protested, "Hey, wait, those are my favorite shorts."

Right after that, one of the doctors explained, "We want to try a procedure first to see if we can realign your neck." It was called a halo, and they had high hopes that it might prevent surgery and be a solution for healing the breaks in my vertebrae. I remember the doctor telling my parents, "You might want to look away for this part." I wanted to know what they were going to do, and they said they had to drill some screws into my head for the halo. Obviously, I was horrified. I got ready for a nightmare of pain when I heard the loud buzz of the drill next to my ear, but it wasn't that bad because I was on so many pain medications.

After the halo was around my head, they attached it to some weights to try to realign my neck. They kept asking me to relax my neck. I told them over and over that I was doing all I could, that I did feel as relaxed as possible. But my neck was so muscular from all the months of hard training for football that they couldn't get the bones to line up again despite several tries.

They took me in for surgery, but I barely remember that. In fact, when I came around afterward, they told me I had been in surgery for nine hours, and I was amazed.

Reality struck when the doctors came in and told us I was paralyzed from the breastplate down. The first thought I had was, 'I'm not going to practice tomorrow, obviously.'

The doctors' voices faded away as they talked with my parents. I was too busy thinking about this new reality and what I was going to do about it to listen to any more details about what I couldn't do. It was too hard to focus on the faces of all the people in the room since my head and neck were in a brace. I could only stare up at the harsh bright ceiling lights. I felt like a piece of furniture with everyone talking about me as if I wasn't there.

My dad had his hand on my shoulder, and I could tell he was fighting back tears. But he leaned over so that I could see his face. "Remember I told you that everything was going to be all right? Even though your body is hurt, you still have your mind and your personality."

Being 18, I didn't have a lot of responsibilities yet, and my life was all about school, family, football, and girls. I had played football my entire life, and I understood how serious this was, but all I could think about was that I couldn't play football anymore. Football had been my life since I was 7 years old. What was I going to do?

The first day after that talk was the lowest for me, as it began to sink in that I was really paralyzed. The doctors didn't hold out much hope that it would ever improve. But once they told me I wasn't going to die, I decided not to cry about it and to be a man instead—accept it and push through it. They told me what I couldn't do, but I wanted to find out what I *could* do.

So, I rallied right away. I had that brief taste of defeat, but I credit my support system, my family and friends, with helping me focus on hope. My football coach used to say, "The man who says he can and the man who says he can't are both right. Which man are you going to be?"

I was going to lose momentum toward my goals—that was very evident. I was going to miss at least my entire freshman year, orientation, football season, and spring break at Daytona Beach with my friends. I was going to miss out on the life I had planned. I knew I had to really train my body and get better so that I could get out of this hospital and back to my friends and family, to the people I love.

We had a family talk about the long list of all the things I wouldn't be able to do. I watched my mother's expression change from fear and confusion to the look of strength and determination that I knew well. It matched my own feelings and my dad's, so we all agreed that we wouldn't let the list stop us.

People had been telling me that I couldn't do things all my life, and I had proved them wrong. We had no intention of giving up.

After the first surgery, the surgeon came in to talk with us. He said, "On the operating table, I tried to think of everything I could do to fix you without surgery. I felt like I was looking at a machine when I looked at your physique. You were in such great shape, your muscles were so defined—I hated to cut you open."

After a day or two of rest, the doctors realized that a second surgery would have to be done to make my neck more stable.

"I'm sorry," the lead doctor told us. "We will have to take you in for another surgery." The look of disappointment on my parents' faces nearly broke my heart. Seeing my mother cry out of anger and frustration was tough, but I just wanted to get fixed up and start working on getting back to my life. My parents prayed with me, and we all asked for a miracle.

I went into the second surgery feeling pretty nervous because I was more coherent this time. They told me they were going to be working near my vocal cords, and I didn't realize they told my parents I wouldn't be able to speak for a day or two.

But against all odds, as soon as I woke up from that surgery, I opened my mouth and said quite clearly, "Where's my dad?"

My parents were shocked and said, "They told us you couldn't speak!"

I said, "Well, I'm hungry. Could I have a McGriddle?"

I was healing quickly from the incisions. After a few more days, the doctors felt there was no reason to keep me in the hospital because I wasn't sick. It was time for me to transfer to a rehabilitation facility.

Prior to the crash, I had been training hard for five months straight for college ball, and all through high school before that. My eye was always on the prize of a professional career in football. How strange it was to discover that I wasn't getting my body in shape for football at all but for all the challenges of physical therapy ahead.

* * * * * * *

Chapter 2 A New Body, a New Life

Slowly working my way up!

One of our close family friends was amazed at the look of determination on my mom's face when he visited us at the hospital. Sure, my parents were scared and devastated, but they were as dedicated as I was to fight for a full, meaningful life in the face of this tragedy. My parents have always been fighters.

It's a testimony to the strength of my family and our faith that we were able to stay positive in response to such a hard reality. I knew a guy who was younger than me, only 17, who had left school to get some McDonald's for lunch and was left paralyzed after a bad car crash similar to mine. His parents had a tough time adjusting to it, and their marriage ended in divorce. So, he was forced into a nursing home at the age of 21. What a terrible thing to endure at that age! But that could easily have been my story, too.

The Fletcher Cleaves Story

After 10 days in the hospital in Jackson, I was transferred by ambulance all the way to Shepherd Center in Atlanta, Georgia. That was a memorable trip, and not for a good reason. I laid flat on my back in my neck brace looking out the back window of the ambulance for six long hours. My mom was in the ambulance with me. She tried to keep me talking, tried her best to help the time pass, but even her strong spirit was wearied by all the hours cooped up in there, waiting and wondering, hoping and worrying.

Somewhere behind us, my dad was following in the truck, driving all of our stuff to our new destination.
I'm sure he was feeling the same way. We didn't know what to expect. All we knew was that Shepherd Center specialized in spinal cord injury treatment and rehabilitation.

We traveled through some mountains and curvy, bumpy roads. I remember my mom calling out to the driver, "Hey, slow down a little. We have precious cargo in here!" The paramedic in the back with us would smile every time she said that.

We left in time to arrive around dinnertime, but Atlanta had experienced a heavy storm. By the time we got to that area, a lot of the roads had flooded, and we had to take alternate routes. The ambulance slowed to a crawl, and I forced myself to stop thinking about the future because it was making me too anxious. How would it be at Shepherd Center? Would I find a way to do my best there and gain some control over this strange, new body of mine?

To keep myself steady, I started thinking about the past, about all the people and events that led me up to this crossroads in my life.

My parents and my grandmother were always my rock, and I can remember even from a very young age, they always told me to never give up, never let anybody dictate what you can do with your life. My grandmother especially was a model of strength. She dealt with her husband's early death which left her as a single mom until she remarried, only to deal with losing her spouse again in her 50s. I was her only grandchild, and she was always there to comfort and encourage me.

Any time I came up against an obstacle, they never coddled me or tried to fix it for me. Sometimes an only child is doted on and spoiled, but not me! They encouraged my natural competitiveness, and I didn't have to look far for someone to test my skills against.

When I was 8 or 9, my cousin Elliot Perry was in his late 20s. He was in the NBA, and before that, he was All American at the University of Memphis. He was the number-one sought-after basketball player in the country when he was in high school. But people had always told him that he was too short to make it to the NBA because he was only 6 feet tall.

He constantly challenged me, despite our age gap. Yet I rose to the occasion every time. If I saw him eating his vegetables faster than me at dinner, I raced to get mine down first. If he jumped off the side of the porch to run to his car, I would leap off the porch and chase after him. He would say, "Hey, if you want to beat me, you have to try harder. Just because I'm bigger and stronger doesn't mean I'm just going to let you win. If you want to beat me, you have to get better."

That message fit perfectly with what I always heard from my parents: "Nobody's going to hand you anything in life. You have to work hard for what matters to you." So Elliot and I would have these competitions. It could be anything— foot races, arm wrestling, basketball, swimming, or throwing a football. I remember we used to put a little grease on our fingertips and see who could leave a mark the highest on a wall at my house. My mother was constantly reminding us, "I hope you all are going to clean those marks off my wall!"

Elliot stuck to his word and never just let me win. Then, when people started telling me that I was too small to play football in junior high or hope for a scholarship in high school, all I had to do was look at Elliot and the battle he fought to prove them wrong.

I remember all the people in junior high who looked at me sideways because of my size when I said I wanted to just focus on football. Up until then, I had been involved in a lot of different sports. I wanted to try them all, and my parents made sure that I followed through with everything I started. So, I never just dipped my toe into something and then quit if I decided I didn't like it. I made both the track and basketball teams. Whenever I complained that I didn't want to finish the season, my parents said, "No, you aren't going to start this team, play two games and decide to quit. If you didn't want to do it, you shouldn't have started." So, I stayed in and gave each sport my all.

But there was something about football that drew me more than any other sport. Maybe it was the intensity of the competition or the exhilaration of eluding everyone to run down the field for a touchdown. Once I got a taste of that, there was no question what I wanted to do with my life.

I remember my first kick return in my junior year of high school. I went out there wide-eyed. I had arrived; all my dedication had brought me to my first varsity game. The crowd roared as I caught the ball on the right sideline in the opening play of the game, and I took off heading for the end zone. I knew the hit was coming, and I knew our opponents had a defensive team with some guys who were almost twice my size. But I had learned to shake off those jitters and deal with it once the hit actually came.

There were times the coach called a specific play that was designed for me. As we broke the huddle, I would go up to the line of scrimmage with my palms sweating and heart pounding, knowing that I was most likely going to get hit. There was a strange kind of mental preparedness that I imagine is similar to what a soldier feels before battle. But now I had entered a bizarre new reality completely unprepared. The last thing I ever expected was to be paralyzed from a car crash just four months after my high school graduation.

As I laid there in the ambulance, unable to feel anything from my chest down, I could still feel my arms twitch thinking about catching the ball, hugging it to my chest, and taking off, spinning and weaving to get down the field. I had spent so many years being aware of every muscle and bone in my body, training myself to higher and higher levels of strength and skill. How was it possible that I couldn't feel that anymore?

"Fletcher, you doing okay?" Mom asked.

"Yeah," I said. "I just want to get there."

The Sky Is NOT the Limit

She squeezed my hand. "Don't worry, son. God has you. He's not going to let you down, no matter how things look. Don't ever doubt that, not for a minute."

In our family, doubt was not an option.

My high school football coach, John Dowtin, contributed to this life lesson. "Don't step on that field if you have doubts that you can win." I remembered the intense look of determination on his face that was reflected on all our faces as we listened to him in the locker room. When he gathered the team together at critical moments, the room was full of emotion but quiet as a church service while we hung on his every word.

Some of my best moments on the field in high school had been captured in a recruiting video I used to seek college scholarships. I thought back to all the careful attention given to every moment of that video, making sure it showed potential coaches the talents and strengths I had to offer. I counted on that to offset their reluctance about my height and weight. I wondered if I would ever be able to be part of something like that again, something that I could be proud of, something that could prove my determination to constantly improve myself.

As lights from other cars flashed on the ambulance ceiling, I closed my eyes and imagined myself whole and strong, getting fired up to go out on the field for the last quarter when our team was falling behind. Coach Dowtin would say, "Fourth quarter. You can't give up now!" That's the image I needed to carry in my mind. I knew I was entering a tough battle, tougher than any I had faced running down a football field.

When we finally pulled up at Shepherd Center, it was 11 p.m., hours later than we were supposed to arrive. We were exhausted and discouraged, which was certainly not a hopeful beginning. But the staff members there came streaming out to greet us as if we were long-lost family. In the bright lights of the entryway, their faces shone with genuine delight. It really lifted my spirits, and I was so glad to finally have something else to look at. I noticed a bunch of bronze statues of the Shepherd family there as they wheeled me out into fresh air.

The doctors and therapists at the Center wasted no time. I was moved into my new room with my roommate Tipper, who greeted me the next morning with a Louisiana accent so thick, I almost didn't understand him. He was 18 years old, too, and had sustained a very similar injury to mine while in basic training for the military. I saw Tipper frequently in between my daily routine, and it became a standing joke with us that I'd ask him to repeat himself just to hear his accent. It was pretty funny.

The very next day, I began intensive therapy sessions and evaluations. My parents notified their employers in Memphis about the situation and they both took a month off to be there for me. The crash was in early September, and I didn't go back home until Christmas. That was the first time I visited back home. I was only there for three or four days before I returned to Shepherd Center, where I stayed until May.

But I was never there by myself—ever. My dad's company was moving to Vegas in November, so at the time of the crash, he had already found a new job. His new employers encouraged him to go ahead and take off the first three months to be with me. He was at the Center every day, all day. My mom took that first month off, and eventually she had to go back to Memphis to work. She would work in Memphis for a week, then fly to Atlanta and be there for a week, and then go back to Memphis for a week, then fly to Atlanta for a week, just back and forth.

When I arrived at Shepherd, I was placed in the inpatient center. There's nowhere for family members to sleep, so my parents would drive 45 minutes to my cousin's house to sleep. They would wake up at 5 in the morning to drive back so that they could be there right when I got up, because they didn't want me to be alone. I would be eating breakfast and my parents would walk in, saying "What's up, dude? We're here!"

Therapy was eight hours a day, Monday through Friday. We had different time slots for different things. For the first couple of weeks, I had a lot of training classes to learn my new body. A typical day looked like this:

8–9 a.m.: bladder training
9–10 a.m.: physical therapy
10–11 a.m.: weights or strengthening
11 a.m.–noon: lunch
12–1 p.m.: occupational therapy
1–2 p.m.: cardio or circuit
2–3 p.m.: aquatic therapy
3–4 p.m.: psychiatrist appointment

All new patients were scheduled to see a psychiatrist. We talked about the crash, how I was dealing with it, and how my family was handling it. He must have asked me questions like, "So, how does it feel to have your football career put on pause? Are you doing all right?" a hundred times during those first weeks. But we ended up speaking more about sports because I was never sad, I was never upset, and I was never angry. A lot of 18-year-olds might have been mad at the world and wanted to give up on life. The psychiatrist told me that most people don't respond to a devastating injury the way I did, especially a young man with so much going for himself.

I know he was puzzled by me. He wanted to know how I managed to have this positive attitude. But it was always how I was raised—that giving up was not an option. I accepted what happened, and I understood that I had to step up and find my way with my new situation. My football coach would always tell us, "A scared man is a dead man." So, I knew I couldn't go through this difficulty being afraid and timid. I didn't have the temptation to cry over something I couldn't change. It wouldn't help anything to give in to negativity, so there was only one course of action open to me—deal with it.

After a while, a typical psychiatrist appointment was mostly about football. "Did you watch the game today? How do you like this player, that player, etc.?" Then we would get to the end of the session and he would ask, "How are you dealing with the crash?"

I would say, "I'm good. I'm ready to get better."

The staff people would give me these medications each morning. I asked, "What is this stuff I'm taking?"

"Well, this is for your blood pressure, this is blood thinner to make sure you don't get any blood clots. And this is an antidepressant."

I said, "I'm not going to take that anymore. I'm not sad. Why take an antidepressant if I'm not depressed?"

The psychiatrist eventually let me off the hook. He said, "If you don't want to take it, you don't have to."

I turned all my attention each day to my next goal. Once I really accepted what I could and couldn't do at each moment in time, I worked on short-term goals with my recreational therapist, LaShannon Ali, and with my physical therapist, Ashley Kim. They were 100 percent in my corner about the importance of constantly challenging myself. They understood that I wanted to prove everybody wrong who thought my disability defined my possibilities.

My parents know that the best thing I can do is tell someone I can do something, because then I'll find a way to get it done. It's just how I was raised. And if LaShannon told me about someone else with my type of injury who was now able to put on a pair of pants, fasten a button, or send a text, then that meant I could do it, too. Above and beyond that, I wanted to be the first to do something no one with my level of disability had been able to do yet.

While I was at Shepherd Center, I was surrounded by other patients and staff, and we were all working on getting better, on learning how to cope back out there in the world. It was toughest thinking about seeing people from my life who knew me before. I didn't want to hear them saying things like, "Man, you're moving pretty well for being in a wheelchair and paralyzed!" or "You sure do a lot of chin-ups for being paralyzed." How was I going to convince them that I was still the same guy they knew before?

The Fletcher Cleaves they knew was ready to take on the world. I thought I was invincible. Imagine having that taken away, out of nowhere, for no reason. Maybe it would have been different and not such a huge switch for everyone if I hadn't been so on fire for football. It's different when you decide you don't want to do something anymore. It would have been different if I had said I didn't want to do football anymore before the crash. But instead, it had been taken away from me, and we all knew that. It made the tragedy that much deeper and harder to accept.

Somehow, I had to replace my football mindset with a completely foreign one—being wheelchair-bound is far from a sport. I could focus most of the time on working toward the next tiny goal, but there were definitely moments during physical therapy when I wanted to give up. It was far from easy. Of course, there were times when I cried and asked, "Why me?" But I refused to be defined by the injury.

That's where I found my strength to keep trying. I refused to be that guy who became paralyzed and gave up on himself, just sitting at home. I didn't want people to say, "Oh, Fletcher Cleaves? He was that kid who could have done anything in the world, but then he got injured and didn't finish college." I wanted my accomplishments to outweigh my disability. I wanted them to say, "Oh, Fletcher Cleaves? He graduated from college and has been traveling the world. He has a good job and a career as a public speaker. He was in a bad car crash, right?" I wanted the injury to be second to my accomplishments.

One of the hardest things to control was the disappointment that would flood over me when I couldn't achieve something as simple as lifting my head and shoulders off a mat for even one second longer than I had managed to do all week. I was no stranger to gradual, incremental progress—that's what athletic training is all about. There were plenty of plateaus in my progress as an athlete, but I knew they were only temporary. Before long, I would achieve my next strength, flexibility, or endurance goal, and it would be something that would spur me on to something tangible that I could see in my performance on the field.

Disappointment during physical therapy was much more discouraging, especially because I couldn't feel anything in 60 percent of my body. I had to fight my own emotions all the time. Trying to repair a broken body is so difficult when you can't feel it, and you wonder if it will ever respond. I'm not paralyzed from just the waist down; it's from the breastbone down. My abs no longer work, my triceps no longer work, and my pectoral muscles no longer work.

These were the muscle groups I used every day in physical training for football, but I never realized how much those muscles are needed for just the normal tasks of life, until after the injury. Just like everyone else, I took it all for granted.

"What are we going to work on next?" This was my constant question for LaShannon. She was a great therapist for me because she never made me feel that I couldn't do something. Instead of saying, "You won't be able to use the restroom on your own for a long time," she would say, "Here is what we have to work on so that you can use the restroom on your own." And that helped me more than I can say. I found myself thinking about my future that way. I knew I wanted to be as independent as possible. Instead of thinking about what stood in my way for those dreams, I began asking, "What do I have to do to be able to live on my own?

Meanwhile, as my therapy progressed throughout the months, both my parents ended up losing their jobs. On top of everything they were facing with my situation, they had to worry about finances, too. But they never let me know what was going on, because I had enough to deal with on my own. It wasn't until later that they told me what had been happening in their lives.

I was just so grateful that they would stay there all day. For the eight hours that I would have to do therapy, they would go to their own training classes for caregivers to learn how to help me with my disability. Then we would eat dinner together and watch NBA games or whatever was on TV that night. Shortly after, it would be around 9:30 or 10 p.m., which meant it was time for them to take the long drive back to my cousin's, then drive back again the next morning, doing the same routine over and over.

I appreciate everything they did for me more than I can ever say. It was always a lot easier knowing my parents were with me all day, every day.

The months I spent at Shepherd were transforming me. With such a supportive and creative staff of encouragers, I began to know and accept my new body. But I never gave up on challenging myself constantly to achieve more, to keep growing and learning. Around my birthday, my physical therapist Ashley was teaching me how to use an assistive device to unbutton my pants. She mentioned that no one had ever been able to do that without the device.

That's all it took for me to feel a surge of familiar competitiveness. "Are you saying I can't do it without the device?" I asked her. And she said she had been a therapist for a long time, and so far, no one had been able to do it.

So I said, "Is that a yes or a no? Are you saying I can't do it?" And she didn't want to say no, but I could tell she had serious doubts. "Okay," I said, "It's almost my birthday. How about this for a bet? If I do it, you owe me two dozen Krispy Kreme doughnuts."

She smiled and said, "And what if you don't do it?"

"Whatever you want," I replied. "It doesn't matter, because I know I'm going to do it."

Right then, without any further delay, I worked at it and got it done without the device. It took me about 15 minutes. She showed up a couple of days later on my birthday with a huge tower of doughnuts decorated with birthday candles. I blew out my candles, and everyone on the therapy floor helped me eat them. That was a truly satisfying bet.

Toward the end of my time living at Shepherd, I had progressed so much in all they had taught me that I figured out how to put in and take out my contacts without any assistance. They made a training video for other patients showing how I did that, and they are still using that video today.

* * * * * *

Chapter 3   The Road to Strength

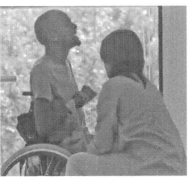

Conquering one small goal at a time.

People often ask me, "Where do you get the strength to be so positive?" I know they're thinking that they could never handle being paralyzed and manage to stay positive. I guess that means they think I'm some kind of superhero or saint. But we all have greatness inside of us. It simply takes the right situation for it to come out. The strength of will I needed to keep from giving up was in me all along. The will is in my spirit.

When I first got injured, I relied on my caregivers and then my parents for everything. And I mean everything. We might as well start with the topic people most frequently want to ask me about but rarely do—using the restroom.

I used to have to set my alarms to go to the restroom every four to five hours. In the middle of the night, school, church, whatever it was, every four to five hours, no fail, I had to make sure my bladder was emptied. It's just something you have to do if you're paralyzed. If you don't, you can get all kinds of complications that could lead to pretty major issues.

I remember setting my alarm for 3:30 a.m. every night, first at Shepherd Center and later back at my parents' house. At the Center, the night staff would come in to help me take care of it. Once I went back to living with my parents, I had to call them for help every four to five hours. Not only that, but every morning after I came back home, my mom would come in to help me get dressed.

Can you imagine being an 18-year-old guy, just starting your own independent life in college, suddenly thrown back to being practically helpless in your old room at your parents' house? Somehow, I had to come to terms with this. Before the injury, it would take me two minutes to throw on some jeans and a shirt, then zoom out the door to school. Every morning in my new body now requires a long, complicated series of maneuvers.

Now I have to stretch my legs to make sure I don't get blood clots. I have to wait for a parent or caregiver to help me get dressed. It takes me 30 minutes to take a shower now with my shower chair. This never-ending inconvenience reminds me every morning how much my life has changed. I can be at the movies or out with friends having a good time, and then my alarm goes off. Same old story—"Sorry guys, I'll be right back."

It's amazing what a human being can get used to. When I first got hurt, I couldn't travel at all because I couldn't use the restroom on my own. I couldn't go more than 30 or 40 minutes away from my parents. I'd go hang out with a friend, then three hours later, I had to be driven back home to use the restroom. If someone had told me in high school that this would be my life, I would have been completely horrified.

If normal life would have stayed "normal," I would have been that guy who sleeps in an extra ten minutes, then runs like the wind across campus lugging a heavy sack of books to arrive just in time for class. Now I can't just jump the curb, cut through the bushes, and weave around the trees. I have to go down the sidewalk and up the driveway or go an even longer way because there aren't any ramps or curb cuts. It was a whole new world, and I knew if I didn't adjust, the wheelchair would get the best of me. This was a battle between the chair and me, and I wasn't about to lose that battle.

The Fletcher Cleaves Story

The natural thing to do in the face of this much trouble is to look for someone to blame. After the crash, the forensics people from the police force tried to locate information about the other vehicle, but they never did find the woman who was involved. Technically, it was a one-car crash since there was no impact with the other driver, so it was hard for them to find her. I could easily hate her for what happened—she had to know what she had caused because anyone would have seen my car fly off the road in their rearview mirror. She had to have seen that. But I'm glad that I'm mature enough that I hope she's at peace about it. That's between her and her God.

The real heroes of this story are my parents. After I was finished with therapy at Shepherd, I moved back home to their house and had some physical therapy sessions in Memphis for the month of June. Then I enrolled in one summer class for the second session from the end of June to August at the University of Memphis. I wanted to ease in with just one class to get used to the campus. This was my first time being out in public in my wheelchair. Then in August, I was a full-time student again.

When I was in college, my dad would do the night routine for me—shower before bed and then the middle-of-the-night restroom trip. My mom got up early every morning to get me dressed and help me with breakfast before she had to leave for work. Then my dad would take me to campus on his way to work. Then my mom would pick me up on her lunch break and take me to her job. After that, my dad would pick me up from my mom's job on his lunch break and take me home to a part-time caregiver until they got home from work. They did some variation of this exhausting routine, day in and day out, throughout my college years.

My close friends are my other heroes. We all think we are so independent, and I was no exception before my injury. I would have been ashamed to ever ask my friends for help. But now I rely on the kind, patient, and constant help of my friends. My re-entry into the social life at college wasn't so easy at first. I've always been a people person, so I always knew a lot of people. Coming back home, many students I had known in high school were in college nearby or were living and working in the Memphis area.

I was a social butterfly in high school—I was well-known for cracking jokes, playing on the football team, and making friends. But going back to college in a wheelchair made me self-conscious and had me wondering if people who knew me before would shake their heads behind my back and say, "Man, look at Fletcher now!"

It turns out, teenagers don't care. They don't care at all, as long as you still act the same, which I did. Then once people started treating me the same, I just went back to being my normal self, telling funny stories, going out, and having fun. Teenagers don't care what you look like—just how you act. My friends treated me the same. They didn't let me give up; they took it on as a group effort.

Around my sophomore year, I started trying harder to be a normal college student going to parties and events, because we all know how important parties are in college, right? I remember this one time, my friends and I were invited to a party. The problem was, nobody told us the party was on the third floor of an apartment building. No elevator. So I said, "Oh well, you guys want to go get something to eat?"

But they said, "No, man, we're going to the party. We didn't come this far to give up now!" So they put me on their shoulders and carried me into the party. One of my other friends carried my wheelchair up, and we had a great time. This was the first of many times that good friends made sure I wouldn't miss out.

I learned to rely on the kindness of friends and family, as well as the kindness of strangers, but I also needed to learn to rely on my own ingenuity and courage. Sometimes, my family and friends expressed concern about my tendency to push myself and take chances. I know they were just worried that I would get hurt, but I figured I had been hurt about as badly as I could be already, so there was no sense in being afraid of any more injuries. I wanted to learn what I could and couldn't do by trying to do as much as possible on my own.

As you can imagine, I was getting impatient about always having to wait for others before I could do anything or get my needs met. Those were usually the times when I was likely to attempt something where my parents would shout out, "Son, are you crazy?!" But I really do hate to wait, and I refuse to accept that I'm as helpless as others think I am. I figured the best way to achieve my goal was to keep going for it, no matter what. As they say, it's better to have tried and failed than never to have tried at all.

The first time I fell out of my chair, I was at my parents' house. I was in my wheelchair, and my dad said, "Hey, I'm going to run to Kroger. Here's the remote, and there's a sandwich on the counter if you need something to eat." I could move my wheelchair around my parents' house pretty well. But he didn't put anything out to drink. He had been gone about 30 minutes, and I was super-thirsty. I figured I could sit there and wait and be thirsty, or I could try to open the refrigerator and get something to drink. At the time, we had a refrigerator with a door handle, and I was not able to pull the door handle.

Time for my critical thinking skills to kick in. I pondered, "How am I going to open this door?" I went to the pantry, grabbed a broom, and tried to squeeze it between the door handle and the refrigerator to pry the door open. That wasn't working, even though I tried different angles. I gave it one forceful yank, and then BOOM! My hand slipped, and I fell over in my chair face-forward with my hands on the floor.

At least I wasn't on my back, so I could push with my hands. But I wasn't strong enough yet to push myself and the chair back up. So I could either stay tipped over like that and wait for my dad to come, or I could purposely fall out of my chair and crawl to the couch. I leaned over, took a deep breath, and said, "One for the money, two for the show, three to get ready, and to the floor we go!" I fell out of the chair and dragged myself to the couch.

My dad came home and saw the chair upside down without me in it. "Fletcher! Fletcher!" he yelled in desperation.

"What?" I couldn't help smiling.

"Where are you?!"

"I'm in here," I called from the couch.

"What happened?!!"

"I got tired of being thirsty, that's all."

That's pretty much when I usually figure out what works and what doesn't work—when I get tired of waiting on people. Sometimes it's a scary thing for my parents, wondering what daredevil stunt I might pull next. For instance, my dad usually dropped me off for my summer afternoon class on his way back to work. The class was scheduled from 12:30 to 3:30, so normally my dad would get off at 5 and come pick me up. An hour-or-so wait wasn't so bad, and I had gotten used to it.

But one day after he dropped me off, I got to the class and the professor informed us that she wasn't feeling well, so class would be ending after 15 minutes that day. My dad was back at work by then and couldn't take more time off. So, there I was at 12:45, facing more than four hours of waiting. That's not how I roll (pun intended), and I decided that I would surprise my friend who worked a little distance from school by wheeling myself over there.

It was all on the same street, from what I remembered, and I thought it was just a straight shot. I didn't know how long the distance was until I measured it later. I thought it would just be a few long blocks.

I took off, rolling down the sidewalk, and things were going well. My wheelchair was half-motorized, called a power-assist chair. I had to use my arms to keep it going. After a pretty long while, I still didn't see the building where she worked yet. I turned around to survey how far I had come already and thought, 'Man, this has been a long way. If I turn around now, it's a long way back.' There was an Applebee's coming up and I considered staying there to wait and get a cool drink. But then I thought, 'That's just too much like quitting. It can't be too much farther.' Once again, it was a battle between me and the chair, and I wasn't going to lose. I kept going.

Then I ran into my first obstacle. Somebody had left a tire in the middle of the sidewalk. I couldn't move the tire, and I wasn't about to turn around and go back after all the effort to get that far. So, I took a chance and went through the grass to go around it, which is not the easiest thing to do in a wheelchair. It's pretty easy to get stuck in grass.

I made it through that trial, and I was pretty proud of it. Then came a more serious obstacle on Sycamore View. The sidewalk ended right on the entranceway of a ramp leading to the highway. The sidewalk did continue, but the curb cut was 30 feet further uphill on the ramp itself.

The chance of getting hit by a car that would be speeding up to enter the ramp was a real consideration. I had to stop and scope that situation out for a while. I looked at my watch and calculated. It was after the lunch hour in the summertime. I had been pushing for an hour now. I thought, 'Surely I'm almost there.' So I made a Facebook post about everything because I thought it was funny. I was positive that once I got up that ramp and back down the hill on the other side, her office building would be right there. I decided to go for it.

I made it to the sidewalk without any close encounters with speeding cars, but I forgot about the big apartment complexes that came before my friend's office. I took a little breather and set off again. That's when I met my third obstacle. I rolled down a long stretch of sidewalk, but then it just abruptly ended. Maybe the construction workers got tired of putting in curb cuts. No curb cut in sight, nothing. Everybody else could just step off the curb and cross the street, but I had only two choices—try to jump it or turn around and go all the way back to the last curb cut and push back up into the street, taking my chances with traffic.

If I jumped it and didn't make it, I'd be in a heap on the pavement in the middle of the street. That was too daredevil of a move, even for me. So I decided to push down my inner BMX and turn around, go all the way back down the sidewalk to the driveway of the apartment complex, and push back up the street. By now, the summer heat and all that exertion were starting to get to me. My arms felt like jello, and my shoulders were aching in protest.

I finally made it past the apartment complexes. I saw her office building. 'I made it! I'm here!' I thought to myself. That's when I met my final obstacle. It happened again—no curb cut. I had to turn around and go back down the street, cross the street, push myself to the nearest light, and go back to the curb cut on the other side of the street. When I finally arrived, it had taken me three hours to go four miles.

My friend answered my text and said, "I'm about to wrap things up. It's almost 5 and then I'll come pick you up at your school."

I texted back, "Well, I'm outside your building."

"Fletcher! You did NOT push yourself all the way down Sycamore View!"

"I did! I got tired of waiting."

You really don't know what you can do until you have to do it. When I told my parents about it, they were not pleased. They said all my choices had been extremely dangerous— going through the grass around the tire; navigating a wheelchair down Sycamore View, one of the busiest streets in Memphis; going up the interstate ramp; and pushing up the side of the street by the apartment complexes. This was another of those times when I got to hear them say it again: "Son, are you crazy?!"

"Hey, I did this, though! Originally, I was going to stop at Applebee's when I hit the one-hour mark. But then I thought, 'This will be one hell of a story if I make it.' I didn't want to give up."

My parents did not seem to share my excitement about my victory over the chair. But I understand how they felt. I am their only child, and they had already lived through one nightmare injury with me. It's no surprise that they weren't thrilled about the possibility that I might get hurt again.

But the hardest thing for me in college wasn't getting from point A to point B, or even the coursework itself. It was the fact that I can't write or type quickly. So, I had to rely on a note-taker. Students who were in my classes were hired by the university to take notes for me. Most of them did it to fulfill part of their scholarship agreement. They took notes in a carbon-copy notebook and gave me the copy.

But it became a problem when the note-taker didn't show up to class or fell asleep or thought something wasn't worth writing down when I thought it was important. It was hard to get the benefit of notes that weren't my own notes.

I could call up a note-taker and ask, "Hey man, are you coming to class today?" Sometimes I'd get an answer like, "Oh, I thought I told you. I'm leaving early for spring break." And there I'd be—stuck without notes that day.

I took my studies very seriously. When note-takers failed, my professors did everything they could for me, and they were understanding about the obstacles I faced. I didn't want special favors, though, and I worked hard to measure up just like any other student. For exams, I would be in a testing room by myself, and I would take the test verbally with a scribe writing down the answers I gave.

I can type one letter at a time using an adaptive keyboard, but of course, it takes a lot longer. I normally needed extensions to be able to hand in my papers, but I got them done. I tried voice-to-text software, but I preferred typing it myself rather than cleaning up all the annoying little errors.

College was going well, and it soon became time to choose a major. It's funny, but the story of my life goes like this: Just tell me I can't do it, and I will find a way to do it or keep on trying. I was always good at math, and I wanted to do engineering, but for some reason the state wouldn't pay for that major because of my disability.

I didn't know what I wanted to do, so my advisor said, "Since you like math, do you want to be a math major? You can be a professor." I couldn't see being happy in an academic environment. Then we talked about computers, and she signed me up for a computer science class.

When I told people I was considering a computer science major, they looked at me doubtfully, just like they used to in junior high school when I said I wanted to play football. "Are you sure you want to do computer science?" they would ask, with their eyebrows raised.

My friends at school said, "That's a hard major, computer science!" But I told them I didn't care—anything valuable in life doesn't come easy. Were they telling me I couldn't pull it off?

I went to my advisor to tell her I was interested in that major. When she also said, "Are you sure you want to do that?" I immediately made up my mind. "Yes. That's my major." And like it or not, I was going to get it done. Even though I knew nothing about computer science, I knew I wanted to take on this challenge because people thought I couldn't do it.

It turned out that I didn't really like it that much, but by the time I was sure of that, I was one class from graduating. So, I finished it, and I'm glad I did. I liked the challenges, critical thinking, and problem-solving. That's what a lot of computer science is—problem-solving. I just wasn't sure I wanted to do it for the rest of my life.

Another high point in college was when I joined my fraternity, Omega Psi Phi Inc. There was a void in my life after my injury because I had always been part of a football team. It was like being in a big family full of brothers. We were together practically every day for practice, encouraging one another through all the training, running the plays together, and becoming a unit. When I wasn't able to play football anymore, I was looking for that brotherhood that always held a deep value in my life.

One of the reasons I joined that particular fraternity at University of Memphis was that when I was in the hospital right after the crash in Jackson, a young man I didn't even know came to see me to offer me encouragement and friendship. I was so impressed that a complete stranger would be so kind. I noticed the Greek letters on his shirt and asked him about that. He told me about his fraternity.

When I got to school in Memphis a year later, I joined that chapter of Omega Psi Phi Inc. and those guys became my new brothers. They treated me like they knew me my whole life. There were scholarships, perseverance awards, and determination awards—so much encouragement and support. Just like my old friends from grade school, they were always ready to do whatever it took to include me.

If they were all going to Nashville together, they'd ask me to go. I told them I wanted to, but I was afraid it would be too much of a burden for them with all my limitations. They would always say, "If you want to go, you're going!"

So many things were starting to come together for me during my last year of college. One of the most significant events was getting my truck. I remember that I was at the dealer talking about which kind of vehicle could be customized for my needs. They wanted to know what I'd rather have—a van or a pickup truck.

"Excuse me? A pickup truck? Yes, please!" I replied. What type of 22-year-old stud like me wants to drive a van (wink, wink)?

I was so excited to have the independence to come and go as I wanted without asking for or needing a ride. The truck was paid for by Vocational Rehabilitation to help disabled people return to work or school. It was a two-year process of filling out forms before we finally got the funding. I took a series of tests to see how strong my arm and hand muscles were, and how fast my reaction time was, so that they could determine which type of hand controls I would need.

The Fletcher Cleaves Story

Once the truck was modified, an instructor from Florida came up and told me he would give me driving lessons for the truck for four days, and on the fifth day, I would be tested. If I failed that test, he would come back the next year and instruct me again. I was both nervous and determined when the test day came. This was my opportunity at last for a big step toward the independence I so deeply wanted. No more relying on my parents or wheelchair taxis (which sometimes took an hour to show up because there were so few available).

I passed my test and got my certification for hand controls! My first solo ride felt like I was splashin' in high fashion. For the first time since the injury, I could just roam around and hit Taco Bell, go see a friend, or pick up some groceries, and take my time getting home.

For quite some time, I had been planning and saving to get my own apartment.

I told my parents, "When I graduate, I want to move out."

"Son, you're nowhere close to moving out," my dad said.

My mom agreed. "We don't feel comfortable with you moving out. We want to know that you'll be able to handle day-to-day living without needing our help."

"Okay," I said. "What do you need me to do?"

Dad said, "You have to show us that you're strong enough to get in and out of bed at any point. Like if there was a fire, or something like that happened."

"Okay, deal," I said. I could get in and out of bed, but my dad wanted me to get in and out of bed 15 times in a row in front of him while he stood watching, making sure I wasn't getting tired. I started working out and lifting weights. It was a long, slow process.

The next step was to learn how to use the restroom on my own, because at the time I was still relying on my parents every four to five hours. I called my therapist LaShannon and asked what kind of devices they had to help me. She's always been my go-to person for ideas for more independence. She told me I could use a new type of catheter designed for quadriplegics. So I started doing that on my own.

Things were looking up. The summer before my junior year, I had interned at AutoZone in the IT department. When my boss said he wanted me to intern during my senior year for pay, that's when I decided I would be able to move out after graduation. I'd be making money my entire senior year, and I could afford it. I started looking at apartments almost right away after that, because I wanted to be prepared for what I would need. I also figured it might not be easy to find an apartment with the right accessibility.

I wanted to be close to my job downtown. First things first, I needed to find an apartment with a roll-in shower. I called one, then two, then more and more until I had called over 30 apartment complexes because no apartment complex in Memphis had a roll-in shower. Every handicap-accessible apartment had a stand-in shower with a step to get into it. That simply was not going to work for me.

I could spend my own money to convert the bathroom to a roll-in shower, but then I would have to pay to get it converted back to a stand-in shower when I moved out again. I wasn't too interested in that option.

Finally, out of frustration, I wrote a letter to the governor and the senate, informing them that there were no apartment complexes with wheelchair-accessible apartments. They wrote to say they received my letter, but it would be two to three months before they could respond. Nothing ever happened through that route.

At last, I found my apartment, close to my job with covered parking. They said I could move in September after I graduated. It was a one-bedroom apartment with a roll-in shower and all the modifications a person in a wheelchair would need.

The Sky Is NOT the Limit

I had saved and saved, so I bought my couch when it went on sale Memorial Day weekend, and I waited for the Fourth of July sale at Best Buy to get my TV. The stores were holding these for me and said they'd deliver it whenever I needed it. My parents were going out of town the same weekend in September that I had planned on moving. I told them, "Hey, when you guys get back, I won't be living here anymore."

They said, "Whatever! You're not going to move out." I had been talking about it so long, they must have thought I was kidding. They didn't expect me to move out until at least December of that year. But that weekend, I moved out.

I called my fraternity brothers and said, "You guys, I need to get all of this bedroom furniture and my clothes out of my parents' house before Sunday."

They said, "Okay, we got you. Just feed us some pizza and a couple beers."

"Okay, deal!" I said. They moved all my stuff in one evening.

My mom called me that Sunday on their way back to Memphis and said, "Son, where are you?"

"I'm home," I answered.

When she got to their house, she called me again. "Fletcher, where are you?"

And I said, "I'm home!"

"You are not at home because we are at home."

"No, y'all are at your house. I'm home at my house."

There was a long silence. "You moved?" She sounded incredulous.

"Yeah," I said. I was lying in my bed in my own place. And it felt great.

"We're on the way." I heard her talking to my dad as she hung up the phone. "This boy said he was going to move out in two days, and he did it!"

My mom always tells that story when people ask her how determined I am. "Well," she says, "let me tell you about the time he moved out."

Once I graduated college and was off on my own, I was in a much more independent position, and I had a chance to reflect on all the things my parents had done. From waking up at 5 in the morning every day to be with me at Shepherd Center to taking me back and forth to college every day— they had been uncomplaining, selfless superhumans. I couldn't have become the successful man I am now without all the sacrifices they made to support and encourage me every step of the way.

Even though none of us had asked for this new way of life, we all committed to it as a family. We decided we were going to work through it and fight through it together. That is why, when I graduated college, instead of asking them for a gift, I gave them an all-expenses-paid trip to Hawaii. They had always wanted to go there but never could because of my injury. That was one of the best gifts I ever gave myself—the chance to thank them at last for all they had done.

* * * * * *

Chapter 4 Interdependence = Independence

From middle school classrooms to college auditoriums.

The first time I formally spoke in public in my wheelchair, I was so nervous. We had a banquet after my injury to raise money for my medical expenses, and my family warned me that I needed to get up and say a few words. I worried about how people would see me and how I was going to hold a microphone on my own. I did it, and somehow, I lived through it. Little did I know it was the prologue to my destiny. Over the last nine years, I've become accustomed to being in front of crowds as large as 800 people with much less fear.

It all started while I was still in college in Memphis. My cousin Elliot was heavily involved in the community through his fame in the NBA, so he was mentoring some young men. One day, he said, "Fletcher, I want you to speak to these kids about what you deal with in life, how you didn't let it dictate who you were going to be, and how you didn't give up on yourself." So, I spoke to the group, and it went really well. I was impressed by how closely they listened and by their thoughtful questions, and I was pleasantly surprised by how much I enjoyed talking with them.

Soon after, Elliott had another group of young men he wanted me to speak to. A man who attended that talk asked me to speak to his son's football team. From then on, it seemed like a snowball effect. Soon, I was speaking at different places and community centers, to basketball teams, YMCA organizations, and school groups.

My biggest opportunity came when a childhood friend of mine called and said, "I work for AT&T, and they're doing a national program on distracted driving. They're going to be at this school, and I want you to share your story with these high school students." When I spoke at the school, an AT&T director was in the crowd. It's funny how God works.

"Fletcher, you need to be on our team—you need to do more of these speeches informing everyone about the dangers of texting and driving. I love it," the director said. And that's how I became a spokesperson for AT&T about the dangers of distracted driving. A year went by before I heard another word from the director. Then out of nowhere, he gave me a call about an opportunity to be on a six-minute short film produced by AT&T and ESPN that would be aired on *College Game Day*, a show on ESPN. As a former athlete, I had always dreamed of being on ESPN. I thought it would be for football, but it turned out to be for a much greater cause.

After the short film came out, I was asked to speak at colleges, churches, and special events for other organizations outside of Memphis. A month after the film aired, ESPN flew me and my friend to New York City where we had a chance to experience Times Square for the first time. Two days later, they drove us to Bristol, Connecticut, to tour ESPN headquarters.

Just as we walked into the building, the director told me, "By the way, you're going to be on SportsCenter in an hour." He wanted to surprise me and also make sure I didn't get too nervous ahead of time. Growing up, I watched that show every day to catch the highlights of the sports world. I couldn't believe that I, Fletcher Cleaves, was going to be on the actual SportsCenter!

They went to a commercial break after some golf highlights and moved me next to the announcers. They introduced me as a young man whose tragedy had turned into an important message for everybody about safe driving and overcoming adversity. I was so excited and nervous at the same time, with so little preparation for this overwhelming moment, that I actually said the AT&T campaign slogan backwards. On live national TV, I was supposed to say, "It can wait. Keep your eyes on the road and not on your phone." What did I say? "It can wait. Keep your eyes on your phone and not on the road." What???

I didn't realize I had said it that way until I was off the air and the director asked me, "Do you know what you just said? On live TV?"

Maybe that could have been something that ruined me for life, but I figured there's no point in crying over spilled milk. By that time, the director and I were friends. I looked at him and smiled. "Well, you're the one who only gave me an hour's notice, right?"

I was so sure I would be in the public eye as a football player. I based my entire life on it. This career as a public speaker was a complete surprise to me, but in some ways, it's not that different from football. I am a member of a team with a mission—to educate people about the dangers of texting while driving. I practice and train for each speech, finding out what my particular audience is like, what they can relate to best, and what the "coach" (the person who asks me to speak) wants me to focus on. In the process, I get to meet so many fascinating people and hear their stories.

The Fletcher Cleaves Story

The best thing is, I am just being myself, doing what I love most—connecting with people. I always crack a joke the first thing. The people who follow me on Facebook see pictures of me facing the crowd while the camera is behind me, so they can see what I see from the stage. It's all about the people in the audience, not about me. How can I give value to them? How can I share what I have experienced in a way that spreads hope and gives them something to consider that might improve their future?

The first thing I typically say is, "Life is all about choices. The choices we make today will affect our tomorrow. What that means is, today, we all have a choice, and we all have positive or negative consequences. My mom always told me, don't let one bad decision give you a lifetime of consequences."

I often talk about a couple of guys I've met at different speeches. One was convicted of reckless driving while texting, and the other was convicted of drinking and driving. They both ended up killing someone as a result, and I share with my audience how one text or one evening's bad decision gave them a lifetime of consequences. They are registered as felons, and different states have different prison sentences and fines for vehicular manslaughter and criminal negligence. But even worse, they have to deal emotionally and psychologically with the fact that their mistake meant someone would never see their family again.

I speak to groups of adults, too—not just to young people in schools. The dangers of texting and driving are almost equal between adults and students, because adults have been driving longer than they've been texting and they think they can drive effectively. Kids have been texting while driving forever, so they think it's perfectly natural.

I tell my audience about studies showing that the human brain cannot do two cognitive skills effectively at the same time. We're not doing two tasks at the same time, even if we think we are. What our brains *can* do is switch between tasks at astonishing speeds, so that feels as if we are doing two tasks at the same time. But we're actually just switching back and forth between texting and driving. We can text and then switch to driving so fast that we think we are successfully doing both at once, but we can't do it.

People often say, "I bet it's so cool to travel all over!" And it really is, but when you are on a paid speaking circuit, you're on their schedule. They might say they need me Thursday at 8 a.m. for a meet-and-greet, then at another venue after the presentation to answer questions. That means I would need to leave Wednesday after work to catch an evening flight, get to the hotel, get something to eat, go over my notes for that particular group, then get up early the next morning to get breakfast. I would arrive at the venue around 7 a.m. to test the microphone and make sure the slideshow is operating correctly on their equipment.

Needless to say, this is a tough schedule for anyone, but for someone with my lengthy morning routine just to get washed up and dressed, it requires waking by 5 or 5:30 a.m. Following the speech, I would need enough time to travel back to Memphis to get to my regular job the following day.

At this writing, I have given around 400 speeches. I've been to speaking engagements as far away as Florida, Louisiana, Texas, Washington, DC, and Colorado. I've met so many people and heard so many different stories. It's just amazing to me—I love it.

It's a lot of running, getting to this hotel, getting to that venue—it's not just hanging out. I remember one time I went to Florida for an evening speaking engagement. I arrived around 1 p.m., spoke that night, and then had to travel back to Memphis for work the next day at 9 a.m. Luckily, there was a flight leaving Orlando, Florida, at 6 a.m. I landed in Memphis at 7 a.m. and got to work by 9 a.m. So, my friend and I woke up at 4 a.m., on just a couple hours of sleep, to catch that flight. It was tiring, but it was definitely worth it.

Another time, I had three speeches a day for two days in a row in Louisiana. That experience was even more grueling. Our team of three speakers went to six high schools in two days. We arrived the night before and spoke at a summer camp where they were putting on a "Choices" program. The program taught that life is about choices and the challenge of making the right choice. Then we started at the high schools bright and early the next day.

Our first speech started at 7:45 a.m., then we drove to the second school to speak to them right after lunch. We traveled to the last school to speak at the end of the school day. It took over two hours for all three of us to speak each time, so we had a very short break in between. We went to dinner, then woke up the next morning to the same thing— three different high schools in one day.

The limited time was definitely a lot of pressure, because we wanted to answer the students' questions. We'd say, "We have enough time for three questions." And there would be 45 hands in the air.

I had another big presentation at the University of Central Florida sponsored by State Farm and CBS Radio. A friend of mine worked at the university where they created an event called Safe Knight Week. It was scheduled the week before spring break, so they brought me in to discuss safe driving and making smart choices. State Farm, one of the sponsors, had representatives there. That was a good experience!

I also gave a speech at the AutoZone headquarters in Memphis and at the National Transportation Safety Board in Washington, DC. Many of the other speeches I've given have been at churches and high schools. The speaking donations and fees I received over the years made it possible for me to save up for one of my biggest dreams—to travel to other countries.

My parents taught me the discipline of saving money early in life. My father especially would tell my mother not to come to the rescue if I needed money. He wanted me to understand that I shouldn't rely on others to take care of my needs. If I wanted something done, he made sure I found a way to get it done myself. Hearing that message in my childhood made me forever cautious, double-checking that I have everything—that I have enough gas in my car and enough money in my account.

If my parents did everything for me growing up, then I wouldn't be as independent as an adult. I've always been good at saving and managing money. In 8th grade, I had $280 stored in my room from carefully saving my weekly allowance of $10, so you can see how frugal I was. My parents got me a debit card, because they said I had too much cash in the house. They taught me how to keep track of what was in my account and balance my checkbook. I thought it was the coolest thing to have a debit card. I'd be at the movies with my friends and they would all use cash, but I would pull out my debit card. And my friends were so impressed. "Wow! That's so cool!" they said. And I replied, "I know! All my money is on this little plastic card!" It was pretty funny.

This ability to save came in handy when I was first on disability in college. I was getting about $300 a month and I learned to survive on that. As college students, we wanted to go out to eat and get fast food every day. But I couldn't do that and have anything left in savings. That taught me extreme money management skills. I knew I wanted to travel, so I started back then, and I still have a constant mindset to save, save, save. Now, when an opportunity to travel comes up, I'm ready to go for it if I want to.

People ask why I travel so much, and I tell them it's because I save up for it all the time! While others are going out to eat and buying clothes, I'm saving. Recently, a chance to go to the Dominican Republic popped up without any advance warning. My close friend was given a free Airbnb there. When he asked, "Hey, you want to go to the DR with me?" I was able to say, "Yeah! When do we leave?" We left that next weekend.

The Fletcher Cleaves Story

I always save for a rainy day. I know I like to travel and I'm very spur-of-the-moment, so I just put things aside toward that. Financially, I can pick up and go whenever I want to, but for safety purposes I don't fly by myself. A flight can get delayed in a city if an emergency happens, like a storm, where no flights are leaving, and I have to stay over. Could I manage by myself? Maybe, but maybe not. I can't always find a friend to travel with, so one of my new goals is working on what I need to do to fly by myself.

I've always been an adventurous person. Growing up, we took a lot of family vacations. My mom and I were the ones who rode roller coasters and took chances on things. But my dad was happy to hold everyone's phones and wait at the end of the ride. When my injury happened, I was 18. I hadn't been a lot of places yet without my parents or under the supervision of some adult. The crash happened just as I was planning trips that I wanted to take on my own.

I told my recreational therapist LaShannon while I was still at Shepherd Center that I loved to travel. She said I should go on a Delta Airlines outing where they teach paralyzed people what to expect on a plane. I really didn't feel like going, but she was adamant that I go. So, my parents and I went there, and it was an eye-opener. It was quite a process getting in and out of the seats, then having someone carry my luggage and escort me from gate to gate.

I hadn't thought yet at that time about road trips and all that I'd have to do for long trips in the car. When you're paralyzed, you can get skin sores if you're sitting in the same position too long. On our first road trip from Memphis to Nashville, we had to make sure to do what's called a weight shift every 45 minutes or so. It involves not only changing position but stretching my legs, moving my lower body around, and inspecting for skin damage. It adds a lot of extra time to a road trip!

My first trip in an airplane after the crash was to Chicago. I was with my parents, and we were pretty nervous trying to remember everything we had to do. It ended up being smooth sailing. Those two experiences helped me gain confidence in myself as a successful traveler. As time went on and I got stronger, my group of close friends who I grew up with started traveling with me and became my right-hand crew.

For spring break one year, a few of them went to Nashville with me because they knew that I couldn't go very far, so they sacrificed their trips. It was my first time going on a trip without my parents. We had a great time there. They helped me with my daily routine—getting dressed, taking a shower, etc. These were things that true friends do for one another. It's rare for a group of friends to be that close, and even more unusual for a group of young adults younger than 20 to be that mature.

You can imagine how strange it could be to have guys I grew up with helping me take a shower. It has to get done somehow, though. It made us all mature a lot faster. It was a great experience, and it helped me realize that things could still be "normal" even in the face of what most people would view as weird. Nothing stopped us from hanging out together, going out to eat, to the movies, or simply just turning up.

After that first trip to Nashville with my friends, I started believing that everything was really going to be okay. People still treated me the same. I was still having fun and still laughing. It made me realize that spring break isn't about where you are, it's about who you're with. I could go into a cave in the middle of nowhere with those friends and still have fun. No matter where we go, we'll still have a ball. To me, every place is fun because I'm with the right people.

The idea of Vegas came up when I turned 21. My 21st birthday was in December, and my best friend's girlfriend at the time was turning 21 the following July. So we all planned for a trip to Vegas after that. For a Christmas gift, my parents bought me and my friend a plane ticket to Vegas so that we could join the group going. That was the first time I went on a plane without my parents. We faced more obstacles than we expected on that trip, but it was a phenomenal time. I was with great people who helped with everything, breaking down my wheelchair and carrying me when we couldn't find ramps or elevators. My friends were never willing to leave me behind. "If we can do it, you can do it," they always said.

If we got someplace and the people there would say, "Sir, we don't have an elevator," my friends' automatic response was "Let's go. How many steps?" And they'd just pick me up and carry me up and down the stairs.

A big travel opportunity came along in 2016—a 10-day tour of Europe through Rome, Paris, and London. At that point, I had been to Vegas many times and had gone on a cruise to Mexico and countless U.S. cities. I had always wanted to travel overseas. This would be the longest I'd been without the aid of my parents. They had been my main caregivers for the past seven years.

Once again, my friends helped me take a shower, get dressed, and get along in a different country. Just try rolling a wheelchair down an old cobblestone street or up steep hills without help! It was lucky my friends were in shape. They took turns pushing me up the mountains the locals call streets. They would complain every day that their legs were tired, and I would simply reply, "At least you can feel your legs! NOW PUUUSSHHH!!!"

I asked the travel agent to call different hotels and make sure they had an elevator or were wheelchair accessible. And they told her, yes, we definitely are. But in Europe, their idea of wheelchair accessible is different from ours here. They had a little motorized chair attached to a rail next to the stairs, kind of like those chairs elderly people put in their house when they can't walk upstairs anymore. The Vatican, our hotel, several restaurants—all had these weird stair-lift things.

But since I am paralyzed, I am in my chair at all times. So I would have to transfer over to the rail death-trap seat, someone would have to carry my chair up the stairs, then once at the top I would have to transfer out of it back to my chair. The entire process would have taken at least 15 minutes. Besides that, this is virtually impossible to do after leaving the nightclub at 3 a.m. on 2-for-1 Long Island Iced Tea night!

We all took one look at that and said, "This is not going to work!" My friends just carried me up the stairs. So there we were in Rome for four days, going up and down those old stairs two or three times a day. I would buy those guys a beer or lunch whenever we went out, to thank them for putting up with such a demanding situation. What did they say? "Don't worry about it. We've known you since the 3rd grade!"

I learned many lessons while in Rome, but one of the biggest is how poorly we eat in America. Literally 90 percent of everything we ate was fresh—from the bruschetta to the lobster pasta to the cannoli. We were at a local restaurant hanging out and eating bruschetta when my friend took a bite and immediately spit it out. The waiter asked what was wrong, and my friend replied, "These tomatoes are super-fresh. They taste like dirt."

The waiter responded, "They are fresh. I picked them this morning in my garden. Americano no like fresh?"

I was crying laughing! We are so used to processed food that fresh tastes nasty!

In Paris, it was a little easier because they had a traditional elevator, so that was nice. It was surreal to be in front of the actual Eiffel Tower when just seven years before, I was a young kid in the ICU in Jackson, Tennessee, wondering what my life would be like. Once I realized I could handle international travel, keep my legs stretched to avoid blood clots, and get around on ancient streets and up and down ancient stairways, I felt like I could do this all the time! So after Europe, we took a trip to Barbados.

The Fletcher Cleaves Story

In Barbados, I wanted to get in the ocean. So, a friend put me on his back and dunked me in the ocean. I'm blessed to have people in my life who won't let me feel disabled. I mean, how many people with paralysis do you know who have actually been parasailing?! Even though the government classifies me as having a disability, my family and friends won't let me be disabled. They share my passion for finding a way to overcome any limitations that might come up.

There have been so many activities that my friends and I would look up online that said "not wheelchair accessible." If we saw that, we knew they weren't talking about me. It didn't apply to us—we were getting into this building or onto that boat regardless. I rode on a dinner boat and even on a jet ski with an instructor.

I had already spent time training in Atlanta at Shepherd Center for this moment. I had told LaShannon that I wanted to jet ski in Barbados. And there I was, sitting behind a guy with a deep Island accent and holding on for dear life. He took off at a high speed, saying something that sounded like "getting gas." The next thing I knew, we were on the other side of the island and I couldn't see my friends. I got a little panicky because I didn't have my cell phone or any way to know if this guy was going to kidnap me or kill me or something. I sure was glad to get back to my friends that day.

After Barbados, we were off to Dubai, and then to the Dominican Republic. You could truly say I was on a roll! Traveling is one of the things that makes me feel like I don't have a disability. I've been to seven countries in the last three years. I like to try different foods and see how other people live. When I got to Dubai, I said, "Wow, this is genuinely almost the other side of the world!" It was a 13-hour flight and we were 9 hours ahead of Memphis. It was just amazing. I truly loved it.

* * * * * * *

Chapter 5   A Father's Vision

By Fletcher R. Cleaves

High school graduation and post-injury vacation.

Fletcher asked me to write a chapter in his book about how this whole journey has been for me. Going back to the day of the crash, I can tell you that it was the kind of day no father could ever forget. Nobody wants to get that call about their child.

I remember it was a Thursday and just another typical day—work, home, dinner. It was the first night of the NFL season, and the first time I'd be sitting down to watch a major game without my son, Fletcher. I missed him often, since he had left early for his first year away at college so that he could train and practice for his upcoming football season at school.

As soon as I sat back in my chair getting ready to watch the game, the phone rang. My wife answered, then she yelled frantically for me to pick up the phone. I could tell something terrible had happened by the sound of her voice. It was the hospital in Jackson, Tennessee, telling us that Fletcher had been involved in a car crash, and because of HIPAA regulations, they couldn't reveal his condition or any information. All they could say was that we had to get there as soon as possible.

Immediately after we got that call, we jumped up. Of course, that was the day I didn't have any gas in my car. We had to get gas before we could take the hour-long drive to him. My wife wasn't very happy about taking time for that! We hit the highway with our flashers on, trying to get to Jackson Memorial as fast as possible. Once we got in the car and started making that drive, I couldn't stop all the thoughts racing through my mind. Was I going to lose my only child? Your mind can be your worst enemy at times, and mine was giving me all these different horrible scenarios. I was thinking the worst but praying and hoping for the best.

My wife kept it all together. She was calling everybody as I drove, letting family members and friends know what happened. I just sat behind the wheel driving as fast as I could while keeping us safe, bawling and wiping my eyes to keep a close eye on the road.

About halfway there, we received another call. It was a number I didn't recognize, but it was Fletcher calling from the hospital. The call came while we were on the highway. I think my tears dried up instantly at the sound of his voice. I was picturing him being kind of mangled maybe. But it was a strong voice, like nothing was wrong with him. Hearing that gave me a tremendous sense of relief, just knowing that he was okay. That calmed me down a lot. My wife will be the first one to tell you that of the two of us, I'm the one who cries easily. I'm the bigger of the two, but the first one to shed tears. She's always been the stronger one when it comes to Fletcher, but what can I say? He's my son.

He said, "Dad, I've been in a car crash. The doctor said I broke my neck."

I was shocked. "What?! Are you okay?" How could his neck be broken if he was talking to me on the phone and sounding so strong? He replied that he was okay and he was in the emergency room now.

Then he asked, "Are you coming up here?"

I almost smiled in disbelief then. Fighting back tears of joy, I said, "Son, if you knew how fast I was going right now . . . Yes, we're on our way. We'll be there in about 20 minutes or so."

He didn't sound like he was in any pain or anything, and he was coherent. I felt an overwhelming sense that everything was going to be okay, no matter what else was going on. Arriving at the hospital, the nurses were expecting us. As soon as we walked in, they said, "You must be Fletcher's parents. Follow us, this way."

There he was on a gurney with a neck brace on. I didn't know what to expect when I saw him. But as I anxiously looked him over, the only scratch he received was a scratch on the back of his hand. From that car flying down a ravine, he only had a scratch on his hand! If it wasn't for the car flipping upside down, Fletcher could have gotten out of it with no injuries. I was relieved to see that his body was not disfigured. My emotions settled from being all over the place. I thanked God for keeping his promise to never leave or forsake us.

The room was small and quiet. He was not connected to a lot of machines, which surprised me. It was cold in there, but he seemed to feel fine. He wasn't in pain or uncomfortable, but I knew his situation was serious.

He looked up at me and said, "I broke my neck." He was in disbelief because he didn't know a person could still be alive with a broken neck. I guess he had watched too many martial arts movies!

It was surreal to hear him say such a thing again. "How do you feel? Are you okay?" I asked.

"Yeah, I'm fine, but I just can't move. I can't feel my legs." Of course, I had heard about that, but I wasn't tuned in to the possibility of paralysis. So, I wasn't really thinking about what might be happening to my son's future. I was just focused on the present—he was alive, and he still had his personality and his mind.

We found out that when his car crashed into the embankment, his neck got slammed into the roof and it crushed the C4 and C5 vertebrae in his neck. I believe we were blessed because he was a very fit guy, really in shape. Otherwise, it could have been a completely different outcome for him. Even though "just" a broken neck is devastating, we could have lost him. But from that point on, Fletcher's world was changed forever.

Fletcher's coaches and half of the football team had already arrived before we got there. Eventually, the whole team showed up at the hospital. The doctor came in to tell us that he was going to try to use a thing called a halo around his head, and they were going to put weights on it. Those weights were supposed to pull his neck back into place. So, we waited, praying that it would work.

But when they came back out with an update, they said he was tensing up. If he could just relax, maybe they could put his neck back into place. But he had gained a lot of weight from working out all summer, and his neck was really muscular. He tried and tried, but it was hard for him to completely release all that muscle. Unfortunately, that process didn't work.

We sat there for hours talking to his roommate Dayne, who had been in the passenger seat of Fletcher's car. Dayne had a concussion along with a badly ripped arm, right down to the bone. Dayne was still very disoriented, and he kept saying the same things over and over: "How's Fletcher? Where's Fletcher? Can I have something to drink? What happened? Can I take this catheter out?" He was not enjoying that catheter!

Dayne and Fletcher were right next door to each other, but they couldn't see each other.

Finally, the doctor came to talk with us. "It doesn't look like your son is going to walk again," he said. I can tell you, that hit like a ton of bricks. I remember Coach Freeze, being a religious guy, went immediately into prayer with us, right there at the nurses' station. It meant a lot to me and my wife to have that prayer time with him after hearing such shocking news.

Even when the doctors told Fletcher he would never walk again, I never saw him flinch or bat an eye. His determination was always there. I could see it in his eyes. His expression said louder than words, "I'm going to beat this." That night was a very long night. By this time, it was around 1 a.m. and the staff told us they were scheduling him for surgery first thing in the morning. They gave him some medicine to relax.

Even though Fletcher was coherent and could talk, my mind was all over the place. It's overwhelming and devastating. You can pray and hope for the best, but you just don't know. The emotions we all went through that night were beyond intense. What was the surgery going to be like for him? How was it possible that he would never walk again? What was our life going to be like since Fletcher couldn't walk? We had no idea how to care for someone with paralysis.

The hospital had a place for family members to stay, and they took very good care of us. It was like a conference room with beds, so other families who had loved ones in the hospital were also there. They had showers set up for us and gave us three meals a day and snacks. Friends and family showed up, bringing us clothes from our house. We stayed there for about a week. It was such a blessing for us, because there was no way we were going to leave the hospital when he was in such a dangerous condition.

They took him into surgery the next morning and put pins in his spine, at C4 and C5, and fused them together. That afternoon they came back to us and said something didn't look right, so they had to get him back into surgery. This time, they were going to go through the front, and they were going to be right next to his vocal cords.

They said he probably wouldn't be able to talk for a few days or be able to eat. A couple of hours after surgery, they said, "Mr. Cleaves, your son is calling for you."

I said, "I thought he wasn't able to talk."

"He's talking!" they said, and they looked as surprised as we were.

When I walked into the recovery area, he said, "Hey Dad, I want something to eat!" He was not only talking; he wanted to talk to everybody. By this time, the whole family and the whole football team were there. A lot of friends and family were there at the hospital with us, and he wanted to see everybody. He wanted everyone to know that he was going to be okay. He acted as if the paralysis would only be temporary, and I think he truly believed that. In fact, he continues to believe that he can make a full recovery. We all believe that is possible.

The doctor came in and talked about the surgery and went over the things the medical staff needed to do. And Fletcher said, "Okay, but when can I start my therapy? When can I start working out again?"

"Son," the doctor said, "You just had major surgery. It's going to be at least a few weeks!"

The hospital experience in Jackson seemed to pass by in a blur. I came home for the first time the final night that they were going to move him from the hospital to Atlanta in the ambulance. I packed luggage for myself and my wife to take to Atlanta.

At Shepherd Center, we saw plenty of people in worse shape than Fletcher. Some were paralyzed from the neck down— they could only blink their eyes and couldn't speak. Other patients had head injuries and had to sleep in a mesh tent over the bed that zipped from the outside to keep them in the bed, because it was dangerous for them to get up due to their brain injuries.

So, in comparison, we were really blessed that Fletcher was able to move his hands, his wrists, and his arms.

That allowed him to go on and still be a productive citizen in life. He's an amazing kid—he's my son, but I'm very proud of him and inspired by him as well, because this guy does not quit.

He was always the smallest guy on the team, no matter what sport he was in. At first, he wouldn't play much in practice because the coaches would look at him and say, "This guy's too little." But by the third or fourth practice, Fletcher was one of their favorites. He had this winning personality, and he was determined to win in every situation. Of course, he lost some games, but the effort he gave made the coaches recognize him. There are hundreds of people going through the same thing as Fletcher, but not all come out with the same mindset he has.

There was a guy Fletcher met who was a year or two younger. He was injured as well, and though he had more mobility than Fletcher, he didn't have the determination to continue with life and keep moving forward like Fletcher. He's currently a young man living in a nursing home. I'm so grateful that Fletcher has the faith and the push to stay on a positive track.

Fletcher has always been the leader of the pack. He will always push himself to the limit. I remember as a 10-year-old, an older cousin of his had a fence he would jump over with no hands. And I'd say, "Okay, Fletcher, face it—you can't jump over that fence like he did. He's 20 years older than you!" Fletcher couldn't do it that day, but in a year, he was able to jump that fence with no hands. He practiced and practiced until he could do it.

Whenever he was in school events, he was the showman. He played the bass in elementary school. After his class finished playing their recital piece, Fletcher hit the bass two more times as if to say, "Look at me, I have this bass, look at me!" His teacher gave him a reprimanding look, and he said, "I just wanted everyone to know that I have this bass, and I can play!" He's just that type of person. We could have called him a "bad kid," but he wasn't a bad kid. He was very active and full of energy.

They suggested we give him Ritalin when he was a child. For a while there, they wanted to give Ritalin to every kid who wouldn't sit still in his chair. And we said, no, he doesn't need Ritalin—he just needs a stern hand from the right person. Whenever he was in a crowd with a bunch of kids, people would notice Fletcher. There's no stopping his energy and enthusiasm.

He didn't want to be the run-of-the-mill type of guy. I remember in high school, ninth grade, we told him that he needed at least a 3.0 GPA, and he said okay. He knew that the better he did in school, the more freedom he'd have at home. Every report card period he would bring home a 3.0 or higher.

He told us afterward that he would pick two classes he could get an A in, a B in, and a C in. And that was his goal. He just needed to keep his parents off his back and make at least a 3.0. He scoped the teachers out and considered their reputations. If he sensed he could make an A in someone's class, or if he knew that a teacher would be difficult and he would probably make a C in her class, he added those factors up to make sure he hit his goal. And I said, "Dude, who thinks like that in ninth grade?!"

He never wanted to do what all the other kids were doing. I called him an outside kid because the video games were getting big when he was growing up. I bought him some games, but he never got into them, which I was very glad about because they were expensive! Instead, he always wanted to go outside and play basketball or football, ride his bike, or go to a friend's house. Trampoline, swim, you name it—he never wanted to sit in front of the TV for hours. He always wanted to be on the move and doing something.

Now that his physical abilities are restricted, he still has that inner drive: "I have to do more than just sit here." He never followed the crowd, and I never worried about him getting into any real trouble. He knew right from wrong, and he didn't want to go down that path. He would see friends getting into trouble, and he would say, "Why would I do that? Why would I want to jeopardize my future when I can just play all day and have a good time?" And his friends would be like, "Yeah, you're right! Why would we do that?" He's always been a leader.

Even when he was in therapy at Shepherd Center, the staff people would say, "Okay, Fletcher, you did a lot of work this morning. Go eat lunch, take a break, and rest." There was a house similar to a Ronald McDonald house connected to the hospital therapy place there. Though he was supposed to take a nap, he would go sit on the deck and talk with other people who had been in therapy. "I don't want to sit in this room all day. I don't want to be inside all day," he'd say, even though I urged him to rest and recuperate.

He would just keep going and going. He can talk to anybody. There wasn't a room he could go in where he couldn't find someone to have a conversation with or interact with, one way or the other.

When we got back home from Atlanta, he registered to go back to college. He was worried about the people his age who had started college, that they were going to graduate before him, and he didn't want that to happen. So, he went to school year-round since he missed a whole year because of the injury and the therapy. He took classes in two different colleges so that he could try to catch up to everybody else. And we drove him to all of these places.

Just before the crash, my job situation changed. I was given the opportunity to move to Vegas, but I had turned it down, so I was looking for a new job at that critical moment in our lives. That became the biggest blessing, because I was able to spend all that time with Fletcher. Instead of starting a new job, I was with him every day for 14 months, until he was able to settle in back at our house in Memphis.

And all that time, I've never seen him in a depressed state except for one Friday night. There was a party at school on campus, and he wanted to go. His mom was tired, and I was tired. If we took him, then one of us would have to go get him because no one would be able to transfer the wheelchair. I said, "Son, it's already 9. If I take you now, you're going to want me to pick you up at 1 or 2, and I'm tired. If you could just sit this one out...," but he said, "No, I'm going to this party."

He couldn't find any of his friends with a van large enough for his wheelchair. So he called a taxi and said he needed wheelchair services and gave our address, but they never showed up. He called them twice, and the dispatcher said someone was on the way, yet nobody showed up. My wife called and asked why no one ever called him back, and they eventually admitted that they didn't have an accessible taxi available, which they should have told him before. After about 10:30 or 11 p.m., I apologized to him. I just didn't feel like I could take him that late.

He said he was just going to go to bed. And he cried that night. It made me feel bad because it was the first time that I had ever seen him frustrated because of his paralysis. We apologized to him again the next day, and I told him, "Man, I'm an old guy and I gotta rest a little bit. But you're a college kid ready to go out and do college kid stuff." And he understood. He knew how much his mother and I were doing to try to help him reach his goals.

We were so happy for him to get his truck. He finally got it his last year of school, and he was able to attend everything he wanted to attend on campus, being a part of college life like he always dreamed about being.

Most people would not have his patience or his willingness to take chances to find out what he was capable of. We weren't thrilled with some of the risks he took. There was a time when he was attending the University of Memphis, and he was also taking a class at a community college to try to catch up to his peers. On this one particular day, his friend was going to pick him up after school, but his class ended much earlier than usual. So, he decided to just surprise her and push his wheelchair to her job. He didn't realize how far it was, and over three hours later, he finally arrived. We were horrified at the dangers he faced to do that.

We went back over and drove the route he took. We found four major intersections that weren't prepared for people with disabilities. The curb cuts weren't there, but he didn't know that until he got to the corner. So he had to go back to the last curb cut and push his wheelchair in a busy street to get near a curb to get to a walkway. It made our blood run cold just thinking about the chances he took. We thanked God for watching over him because it was so dangerous. Of course, he thought it was funny!

Fletcher and his mom wrote a letter to the city to tell them about that corridor, that the curb cuts were not done. People don't realize how many obstacles Fletcher and others in wheelchairs face. If someone put their garbage can in the middle of the sidewalk, he'd have to go backwards to a curb cut or a driveway, push his wheelchair on the street and then find another curb cut or driveway to get back on the sidewalk. If anything is blocking a sidewalk, if a tree has buckled the pavement, or if it isn't smooth for whatever reason, he has to backtrack to go around that and find another way. I think about what he went through that day. It took a lot of grit, but he did it, and he made it.

In the aftermath of the crash, I prayed the same prayer every day: "God, if You can just take care of this one thing for me, take care of my son for me." But I realized over the months of Fletcher's rehab and his many victories over his disability that God has been watching over him his whole life, so why would He leave him now? It helped me to put things into perspective. I'm so proud of this young man.

I see the young adults he's hanging with today who are his friends, how they gravitate toward Fletcher and ask him what he wants to do. And his friends are unbelievable people. These guys and girls are around 30 years old, and they've known each other since middle school. There are about 10 of them. Even though they went off to college, when they come back home, they're best friends. They've been best friends since grade school, and they are still best friends today.

When he first came home from Atlanta after his six months at rehab, his friends never let him act disabled. They would come over and put his chair in the back of their truck, and he would go everywhere with them. He never became an outcast; he was always still a part of the crew. And that's what they call themselves, The Crew. They still do everything together. We parents know all of them. They come here to eat, and Fletcher goes to their parents' houses to eat.

They go on trips together. Traveling with a disabled person, there are things you have to do to travel with the airlines and taxis, especially with traveling abroad, going to these foreign countries. There are personal hygiene things that he needs. He has a service come in for that when he's home to help him get dressed, take care of bathroom routines, get his food prepared, and all of that. His friends take care of it all when they travel—these kids have no problem with it. That's incredible to me. They never looked at Fletcher differently, and I think that helped him to maintain his way of life.

All through his college years, we were the main caregivers. My wife and I rotated schedules. I'm a night owl, so I stayed up with him at night. We watched sports together, so I helped with whatever he needed to do to get ready for bed. His mom is the early bird in the family. So, she helped him get up and dressed, and got his breakfast ready.

Luckily, my wife and I worked in an office complex where our buildings were right across the parking lot from each other. So I would take him to class in the mornings, and when his classes ended in the early afternoon, my wife would pick him up from class and drive him back to the parking lot. I would take my lunch late, transfer him from her car to mine, and drive him home, setting him up with something to eat and getting his textbooks and computer ready. He would do his coursework until we got home to make dinner.

We organized our lives like that for nearly four years, for every day he had class. We just did what we had to do for our child. We both missed a lot of team lunches and team outings, but we had something more important to do—to make sure our son was able to get his college education. There couldn't be anyone more proud than we were on the day he rolled across that stage. He worked hard and sacrificed a lot for that degree.

During his senior year, when he started talking seriously about moving out, our biggest concern was that the service agencies would not be dependable. If he was living far from us and the service didn't show up to help him in the morning, he'd be stuck there until someone could come to help him finish getting dressed. It would be a big change for him after so many years of relying on us to be there every step of the way.

I had all kinds of warnings for him about moving out. "Son, you really need to think about that. What if this happened, or what if you can't do that, or what if you can't get anything to eat or drink?"

And he always replied, "I'll figure it out! I'll just have to figure it out." That was Fletcher's motto. Still is.

I couldn't imagine how he could handle all his various protocols without our help. But he found what he needed. He talked with his therapist and went on the web, did his research. For instance, he found a type of catheter for people who don't have the use of their fingers. That was six years ago, and he's still using it successfully. He figured it out, and now it allows him to have his independence.

Once he gets help with dressing in the morning, he's good all day. He can undress himself—he just can't button up his clothes or get his belt on in the morning. When he told us that he was going to move, we had 100 reasons why he shouldn't. He had 102 reasons why he should. So, my wife and I went on a short vacation. He told us, "When you guys get back, I'm going to be gone." And we didn't believe he could do it, especially after how long it took him to find an apartment with everything he needed.

The news station even did a story on him because he contacted the city and said there were no places in Memphis he could move to that had handicap accessibility for people in wheelchairs. The lawyers from ESPN who were involved in the short film about Fletcher got together with the lawyers of the real estate company, and they worked out the adjustments he needed in the place where he's living now. They made all the doors automatic, so he could easily get in and out.

I think that was the best move he made in his life, being in his apartment and on his own. He figures everything out as he goes. If he's not sure how an upcoming situation will be, he doesn't overprepare. He likes to be proactive, and he's good at that, but he's also really good at going with the flow and improvising along the way. I admit, I wasn't very happy with him moving out at the time, but he had his degree, he had a full-time job, he was 23 years old, and it was time for him to go. He wanted to hang out late, or he wanted his friends to come over late. We're old people—we go to bed at 9. So, it was better for him to move out. I'm glad he made that decision.

It was hard for us to accept at first because he moved so far away. He's in downtown Memphis, about 30 minutes away from us. He had a few mishaps, but he always came out all right. He fell out of bed one night, and luckily one of his friends lived in the apartment building. Fletcher called him and told him the combination to the lock on the front door. His friend got him up and put him back in bed. He had to do that twice. His friend moved out of the building, but he still came back over to get him back in the bed.

Another time, Fletcher was going to his rooftop, and he pushed the door open. He had automatic wheels on his wheelchair, and the door closed and hit his wheel. Whenever you touch those wheels, they automatically go forward. So when the door closed and hit his wheel, there was no place for the wheelchair to go when the wheels engaged. So that flipped his wheelchair upside down. He got banged up pretty badly.

But another of his friends from grade school, Ashlyn, actually lived in the apartment building too, and she and her boyfriend came up to help him. I think she's a nurse. She cleaned him up because he was bleeding, and he didn't want to go to the hospital. He just wanted to put a band-aid on it.

He really has some wonderful friends. The funny thing about this particular friend is, she and Fletcher were in afterschool care together when they were little kids. Every day, when we got there, she would run to us and tell us everything that Fletcher did. "Fletcher did this today, Fletcher did that today." He did not like Ashlyn telling on him. But now they have become good friends as adults.

* * * * * * *

Chapter 6 A Mother's Perspective

By LaSandra J. Cleaves

Mama's joy.

I'm extremely proud of our son, how the Lord has delivered him and continues to heal him and give him guidance.

The night of the crash, the call came from the hospital while I was asleep, and it was terrifying. At first, I was a little disoriented, so I couldn't exactly grasp what was going on. The person on the phone identified herself as calling from the hospital in Jackson, Tennessee, and told us that our son had been in a car crash. That's all they could tell us because he was 18. They couldn't give us any information due to the HIPAA regulations. I was begging, "Please tell me—is my son alive?" When the woman said she couldn't disclose any information, I became very emotional. "Please, please, tell me. I have to know if he is alive!"

The woman took a deep breath and then responded, "Yes, but you need to get here quickly." When I heard her say yes, I felt like my heart started beating again. Okay, I thought, we can get through anything else, no matter what happens.

My husband, bless his heart, was caught off-guard, and this was the one time he didn't have enough gas. We had to get gas and couldn't find an open gas station. It was a pretty hectic time, racing to get on the highway.

The 60-minute car ride seemed to take forever. We were praying the entire way there. The main thing we did on the drive was call family, call as many people as we could to let them know what was going on, where we were going, and to ask for prayer. We just prayed and prayed. We wanted to get there so badly.

When Fletcher called us, hearing his voice made me a little more calm. He said, "Mom, Dad, I broke my neck. Are you guys coming?"

I said, "Son, oh my God, yes! Of course we're coming, as fast as we can!" We didn't quite grasp how he could have broken his neck but still sound so coherent. It didn't matter to me. As long as he was alive, we could deal with it.

We finally got there. I remember there was an officer waiting as we pulled up to the emergency room. People from his college were already there, so the word must have gone out quickly. Once we got there, seeing him was the greatest joy. He was alive—we could deal with anything else. Our son was alive.

Fletcher was muddy, but he wasn't bloody. I just couldn't comprehend the severity of the crash. Besides being muddy and a couple of scratches, that was all the damage I could see. But when the doctor told us he was paralyzed and he would never walk again, I wanted to tell him, you're not God. Even though Fletcher currently isn't walking yet, no one has the say-so but the Lord.

When they showed us the X-rays of his injuries, the angle showed his earrings and they looked like they were in his throat. "Oh my gosh," I cried, "you swallowed your earrings!" But it was just an optical illusion. They were still in his ears—one of those funny moments. Of all the things to worry about, I don't know why I panicked about that.

We stayed at the hospital the whole time he was there. Near the emergency room were lounges that pulled out into beds. The hospital staff was phenomenal. They actually had organizations and churches come in to feed the families of patients. We had family members and friends who would come. But they only allowed immediate family to visit at first, and I just had to go see him every chance I could. I didn't want him to be alone in the ICU. Of course, we couldn't stay there all the time, but I didn't want him to feel like he was by himself. In the morning, I would tell my husband, "Let's get up and go check on our son."

When we talked to the doctors at the hospital in Jackson, they told us that Fletcher would only be able to wiggle his hands and forearms. He wouldn't be able to raise his arms or use them for anything else. In response to that, we started our own rehab right there in the hospital. We wanted to work on what we could while we waited, since we didn't know how long we were going to be there.

Every hour, I said, "Okay, Fletcher, wiggle your hands," and he would wiggle his hands. If that was all he could do right now, then that was what we were going to do—no sense in giving up. You have to do what you can, with all your heart. Since he couldn't move his legs, we would exercise his legs every hour. My husband and I would rotate—my turn, his turn, my turn, his turn. We figured it was like anything else in life; whatever we can do, let's improve that.

Fletcher had his share of setbacks, of course. The biggest one was not having control over elimination anymore. You can imagine how embarrassing it would be to have any kind of bathroom accident in public, but it happens all the time to people who are paralyzed. It could have been enough to make him into someone who never wants to leave the house, but that's not our son.

The first time it happened, we handled it just like we handle everything else in our house—we all talked about it, but we didn't dwell on it. You can't unring a bell or wish something hadn't happened, so we move on. If you dwell on anything, it will throw you into a depression and give you those dark thoughts. But we just learned to move forward. And that's what he did—we talked to him and he just moved forward.

Fletcher is extremely determined. You could even call him headstrong. If he sets his mind to do something, he's going to do it. He's been that way since he was a little boy. We have learned with Fletcher, now that he's an adult, that we can't control what he does. But even as a child, I thought, this child is just so strong-willed, what can we do to help him not be that way? But that's who he was, as a child and as an adult.

I'm so thankful for my husband because when Fletcher was growing up, he would behave better for male authority figures than for women. It's not that he didn't respect women, but he looked up to a man more than to a woman as a young boy. But once my husband got a hold of him, his behavior would improve right away, like magic. We saw that he would always need a strong, firm hand growing up.

When he was younger, he tried out for a baseball team. After a few practices and one game, he came home and said, "I don't like baseball. I want to quit."

We said, "Well, that's just too bad. If you commit to something, you finish it—period. Then you don't have to sign up again, but if you commit to it, you have to finish."

All that early training became a lifeline for him, and really for all of us, as he faced the huge challenges ahead once he left the hospital in Jackson, Tennessee. The ambulance ride from Jackson to Shepherd Center in Atlanta was our first big ordeal after leaving the hospital, because our insurance wouldn't pay for a helicopter ride to Atlanta. On a normal day, Atlanta is only five hours away. But this was a year of historic flooding in Atlanta, so it took about eight to nine hours to get there.

Fletcher was flat on his back in a stretcher, and I was in the ambulance with him. My husband was driving his SUV behind us, carrying what we needed to bring with us. I remember the road had a lot of hills and some sections of the way were quite narrow, so the ride was full of twists and turns. I had to remind the driver several times to be cautious, because my precious cargo was in the back.

My main concern was not showing any fear because I didn't want my son to worry.

As we got closer to Atlanta, Fletcher heard me talking with the ambulance driver about the state of the roads and all the flooding. I took pictures of it and showed Fletcher what was going on. Periodically throughout the trip, the driver had to keep pulling over so that we could exercise Fletcher's legs and move him around to avoid blood clots. That was the longest eight hours of my life, I think.

Once we got to the rehab center, the team was waiting for us even though we got there hours later than expected. They stayed there and greeted us as we pulled up—that was a heartwarming sight, truly phenomenal!

At first at Shepherd Center, Fletcher didn't have a manual wheelchair, but he had a loaner power chair. That thing went a lot faster than anyone expected. Trying to learn how to work the power chair was an experience. Fletcher could see that if he kept using that power chair, he would never be as mobile as he wanted to be. That's what the staff worked on with him mostly—his independent mobility.

He couldn't transfer from the bed to the chair or the chair to the bed because he couldn't sit up. He didn't have the arm strength. The therapists asked him for his goals. He had a long list.

"I want to be able to sit up, I want to be able to transfer, I want to be able to feed myself, to be able to do everything I possibly can with my new body," he told them. And they taught him. They taught him how to control his torso to the limit of his ability, how to transfer himself, and how to balance himself. It seemed very minor sometimes, looking at his progress from the outside, but it was a big deal being able to throw a ball from his chest outward, even though he couldn't throw it like he used to prior to his injury.

"The more I can do, the more I can become independent," he said. He worked at everything they gave him constantly, just like he used to train for football games. Fletcher was already planning how to be independent a month or so after getting back home to our house in Memphis. He didn't want to live with his parents—he likes the company of his peers and being out and about.

The therapists knew exactly what they were doing, step by step. They helped Fletcher to be patient with his progress, celebrating each milestone along the way. They spent a lot of time teaching us how to help him and what to do when we went home with him. I can't say enough about the staff at Shepherd!

Every single day, he asks himself what he can do to advance. So, I'm glad he's not a complacent person at all, and we realize that risk-taking is just part of that spirit of his. We have always told him, since he was a small child, to be as independent as he can. "Don't depend on anybody—do what you can to help yourself," we taught him. He has always taken those teachings to heart.

I remember when we first came home from Shepherd Center, my mom had a big dinner for the family. We are a very close, very large family. My husband and I told everyone, "You guys, don't do anything for Fletcher that he can do for himself." He had enough control of his torso, even if he slipped down on one side, to have the strength to pick himself up. It would take him about 10 minutes or so to get back up straight in his chair.

The aunts and uncles and cousins wanted to help him so badly, but we told them not to touch him. Now it takes him just a few seconds to straighten up if he loses balance with his torso.

We didn't allow anyone, including ourselves, to handicap him. We always told people to let him do what he can, because the more he does it, the better he will get at it. And people mean well, but they're not always going to be there. No one is *always* going to be there to help him.

We intentionally avoided hovering over him. When the weather was just awful, Fletcher had to decide if he was going to deal with it or stay home. He always chose to go to class, no matter what the weather was like. We would drop him off as close to the building as we could, but Fletcher couldn't hold an umbrella yet. So, if it was freezing cold and raining and there was no walkway with shelter, he would get to class soaking wet, but he would stay there because that's what he had to do.

He could have said, "I'm not going to class; I don't want to be wet or cold." No. When we dropped him off, he wheeled to class. He was cold and wet, and he stayed in class because he needed that class to graduate. If class was in session, he would be there by the strength of his spirit and determination.

Speaking of his strong spirit, Fletcher was taking a summer college class that was supposed to go all afternoon, but that particular day, the class ended much earlier. He didn't want to wait all afternoon for his friend to pick him up after her job at an insurance company, so he decided to meet her at her job by himself in his wheelchair. But there were spots all along the way that weren't handicap accessible, where the sidewalks didn't have curb cuts. When he showed me what he dealt with, including having to wheel himself down the street at points, I said, "Dude, you've gotta be kidding me! You can't do that! I thank the Lord that you have that inner drive and that you're not afraid to try things, but really?!"

That's just another example of how strong his will is. He is always saying, "If I don't try it, how do I know if I can do it?" But he did it.

And when he was pledging in the fraternity, I really thought he had lost his mind, because one of the stipulations of the fraternity was that the parents couldn't help him. So he had to have his fraternity brothers take over whatever had to be done, or the young men had to do it as a group because they said, "I am my brother's keeper." That showed Fletcher's determination again.

"I'm going to pledge. I'm going to do this, and with the help of my brothers, we can do this," he said. And he did, because they would be gone together for hours at a time. In addition, he had to get to class and do his studies. He did it. They did it together. That was one of the things that stood out for me. I was so proud of him for that.

Fletcher's graduation day from college was the best day of my life. It was Mother's Day, and I can't describe the joy I felt. It was the best Mother's Day ever. We joined my cousin in a suite that had a bird's-eye view of the stage. When the graduating class was marching in, and then Fletcher wheeled in, I lost it. I completely lost it. My son was graduating from college!

After what he had gone through, he still had the determination to go back to school straight out of his therapy at Shepherd for five years consecutively, every single month. He attended the University of Memphis as well as a two-year college at the same time so that he could catch himself up to his peers.

I credit Fletcher's response to reverse psychology with his level of success and all that he has conquered with his disability. When anyone would tell him what he couldn't do, his attitude was always "I can show you better than I can tell you! Let me prove you wrong!"

"I'm gonna move out, I'm moving!" he told us after he graduated college. "Oh yeah? Okay, boy, go right ahead," I said, laughing. I really thought he was kidding. My husband and I went out of town and came back, and his fraternity brothers had moved everything out of his room. He already had an apartment and had ordered his TV and furniture to be delivered!

We came back from out of town and the room was empty. I thought, "Wow. He really moved!" I really didn't feel he was ready for that yet, but he was an adult and I couldn't keep saying, "You shouldn't do this, you shouldn't do that," even when I thought he was making a mistake. My husband and I were sure he was joking. But he's a nut—he moved!

The Fletcher Cleaves Story

We also thought he was joking when he started talking about traveling outside the country. When it became clear that he was serious, I was very nervous about him being far away without us. We stressed that he had to be his own advocate. "You know the ADA rules," we told him. "So, don't let anyone tell you no. You stand up for your rights."

I remember his first trip out of the country when he went to Europe. He called us when they got to Paris and said, "They lost my wheelchair, Mom!" Of course, there was nothing we could do from home all the way in America, but I was so worried. The pilot and the crew wanted Fletcher to get off the plane and be transferred into an airport wheelchair because the flight had already been delayed and the next flight needed to board. But Fletcher, being the headstrong person that he is, said, "I'm not getting off this plane until my friend physically sees my wheelchair."

The crew would go back and forth on the plane, panicking, and they kept saying, "WE FOUND IT!" But Fletcher's friend would go look at the chair and say, "No, that's not it." The flight boarding next had to be delayed, so Fletcher stayed on the plane for almost two hours waiting for the crew to find the right wheelchair. Eventually they found it, and everything was fine after that.

Even now, we voice our opinion about his travel plans, but we don't try to stop him. If he says, "I want to go to Fiji," we say, "Then just be safe, and do that." I know it sounds like we're nonchalant. We aren't nonchalant, believe me. We've given him the necessary tools in life to make a decision for himself, and he's an adult now.

When the bird is pushing the baby out of the nest, the baby bird may fall to the ground or it may fly. Fletcher has worked hard for his independence, and I see him making the right decisions and doing what is right. When he's traveling, we ask him to check in with us every now and then when he can. We used to be nervous about his trips, but not anymore.

I was surprised when Fletcher first started pursuing public speaking. Even though he has always been outgoing and the life of the party, I never thought of him in front of an audience like that. But when he started telling his story to groups and churches and schools, I saw that he could broaden his horizons and reach a larger audience. It doesn't surprise me a bit now that he is speaking to much larger audiences and has been on TV.

Every day while he was growing up, we would tell Fletcher, "Remember who you are and what you represent. Everything you do has consequences, consequences, consequences. Good or bad." We quoted that to him on a daily basis. He would get out of the car and run because he got sick of hearing it. He got sick of hearing it, but he still quotes it today at his speeches!

When we talk to other parents now, we tell them, even though our son is in a wheelchair now, even prior to his being in a wheelchair, we made sure not to handicap him. Fletcher's allowance was $2 a day, and if he missed a chore, he lost $2. And if he kept missing chores, this week would carry over to the following week and be deducted. So, he always did his chores because he figured out pretty quickly, that was his income! It was his fun money, cookie money, and movie money.

He learned really quickly to save up. He couldn't spend his cookie money if he wanted to go to the movies on Friday. My husband and I did the best we could from what we knew. It helped, it really helped. We are very thankful, because I don't know if we could have made it if Fletcher didn't have the attitude he has.

People ask, how did you guys do it? I'll tell you, you have to stick together as parents. We've talked with parents whose children have been paralyzed or have been through something traumatic. My husband and I tell them, "One of two things will happen—it's either going to bring you closer together or tear you apart. It's your decision as a family what it does." It's hard, it's still hard, but you just have to keep moving forward. One couple we met got a divorce. I will not tell you that their child's injury was the reason, but I'm sure it contributed.

It's worth the hard work to keep the family together. It is a joy now. We sit together as a family out in the backyard with my husband grilling—he loves to grill! Fletcher is out on his own, driving himself and seeing his friends. We can't be anything but grateful. I am proud of him. Proud, with a capital P-R-O-U-D—with every letter capitalized. Not only proud of his speaking career, but proud of what he can do, because I saw what he went through and what he's battled. Now he's speaking to the public and uplifting others all over the world.

Some people are afraid to ask personal questions, but when they ask, he will answer honestly about what happens to our bodies when we are paralyzed. He doesn't sugarcoat it—he tells his audiences exactly what it's like. He also makes a point that a lot of people need to hear: What is happening right now is just for now—nothing is permanent. You deal with it, moment by moment.

This whole journey for our family could have had a very different result for each of us. For me, it has deepened my faith more than I could have imagined. One day, I know

Fletcher is going to walk! I believe it, I do, I see it! In God's timing. We always want everything now, but in God's timing. That's the perfect timing.

* * * * * *

Chapter 7 A Patient Becomes a Friend

By LaShannon J. Ali, Therapist, Shepherd Center

When Fletcher was first injured, he was in Tennessee, and then he was transferred to us at Shepherd Center here in Atlanta. He progressed to what we call "medically stable" pretty quickly, because he was a young, athletic guy. The younger athletes typically don't have as many medical issues. Our therapy program is five days a week, from 9 a.m. to 4 p.m. where we have our physical therapists, occupational therapists, counselors, and speech therapists. My title is recreational therapist. We have nurses on staff as well as exercise physiologists, and therapy techs.

The Fletcher Cleaves Story

When I first met Fletcher, he was still newly injured. He hadn't gone out into the community yet. I was the first person to take him on an outing with our adolescents and young adults—anyone ages 12 to 21 we put in our adolescent program. Every Friday, no matter where the kids are in the hospital, whether they're in the spinal cord injury unit where Fletcher was, or our brain injury unit, we try to get them out for an outing somewhere. It could be a pizza place like Mellow Mushroom, to the mall or Target, to the movies, or it could be bowling, where a special ramp is set up that feeds the ball onto the lane. Sometimes, we stay at the Center and hold game days, prank-your-therapist day, or watch a movie.

We want to get the young people together on a regular basis because they're all dealing with something similar and at a very young age. The socialization advantage, allowing them to be with people their same age who really understand what they're going through, is huge. So, Fletcher hadn't been out at that point yet because he had only been there for a short time. I took him to Lenox Square Mall in Atlanta, a huge mall, that first Friday. His mother was terrified for him to be away from her for the first time. She said, "I haven't left his side since he was injured. He left me one time to go to college, and I almost lost him."

Hearing her fear kind of made me step back a little bit because as a professional, I don't normally think about how the parents feel. I'm totally focused on improving the quality of life for the patient. I think sometimes professionals don't factor in how significant this whole therapy process is for the parents. And I'm also a parent! My daughter at that time was not even 3 years old. So, I told Fletcher's mom, "I get it. I promise you I'm going to take really good care of him. This is what we do—it isn't anything new, and there will be lots of other kids going."

She was still scared, though. I told her what to pack in his bag and everything. On the outing, Fletcher and I were taking care of things in the bathroom. I didn't shut the valve on his leg bag quickly enough, so Fletcher ended up with a yellow stain on his white jogging pants. "Oh, man!" I said, "I'm going to change those pants for you. Did your mom pack pants?"

"Yes," he said. So, I looked in his backpack, and it was almost like an overnight bag. And I said, "Oh my God, did your mom think you were spending the night at the mall? All she needed to do was put in a pair of pants and the catheter stuff." It was as if she prepared for any possible thing he might have needed, which was sweet and motherly, but was entirely too much stuff. It ended up being hilarious. It's always good when you can laugh about things. When we got back, the rest of the outing was great, because we had made it through the hardest part with humor.

At that point, Fletcher couldn't even lean side to side on his own, he couldn't push his chair on his own, and he was pretty dependent for even basic things like feeding himself. I'm sure he was worried about how it would go on his first outing with me and his first time away from his mother since his injury. That was one of my earliest memories of my time with Fletcher, and I think that's where we bonded. We laughed so hard together that day, and it set the tone for our future work together. We could always count on Fletcher to find the humor in things, no matter what was going on.

These outings are just part of our strategy to empower patients and their families with the knowledge they need to be successful on their own when they return home. For instance, we have apartments at the facility. For any patient who lives more than 60 miles away from Shepherd, we have accessible apartments for the family and the patients to stay in. At first, the family members get 30 days of housing for free, because we get patients from all over the world. That is one less thing they have to worry about if they're coming from another state, they don't know where to stay, or maybe they don't have money for a long hotel stay. And of course, they want to be with their injured family member. This gives them 30 days to figure out a long-term plan for staying at or near the Center, depending on what the patient needs.

We have two programs: one for brain injury and one for spinal cord injury. Patients move into the apartments with their families once they discharge from inpatient rehab and go to one of our day programs. Over the course of the inpatient program, we're training the family to be able to provide care for them, which prepares them to go back to their homes.

So, our apartments are almost like a transition from the 24-hour nursing care, where the nurse is doing everything, to living in an apartment, but right next door to us. This provides a safety net of support while everyone learns what they need to do from us Monday to Friday, 9 to 4, and then the family takes over the care in the evenings and on weekends.

Once they have gone home, our patients make return trips to the Center to refresh their skills and to learn new skills. They sometimes don't know what they need to work on until they have been home for a while. Or they are just not strong enough yet to do the skills that they could handle in six months or a year as they get stronger. The first time around is more focused on really intense therapy—everything is brand-new. The next time they come back, they are more aware of their strengths and weaknesses, and they are much more clear about their next goals. They may be going back to school or working already, or they may want to go to work or go back to school. We help them continue to add skills to be as independent as possible.

One of the biggest factors for success with any patient is his or her attitude. Fletcher's winning attitude shows in his motivation. He was very motivated before his injury, being an athlete and loving sports. I think he took on the challenge of his injury the same way he did with sports. He was a small guy who played football, so people were doubtful of his chances and told him, "You're not the right size for football—you're not going to get a scholarship." But he kept pushing and pushing until he got that scholarship.

He approached his therapy with the same mindset, so I think that's why he was so successful. He saw his disability as a challenge to overcome. He had his days—everyone has their days—but he always came in with a smile on his face, always joking, always ready to do the work. That made us want to push him just as much as he wanted to push himself. He's very personable. He always wanted to engage and get to know all about the people he met.

I'm with these patients at the Center every day, and I definitely see the mental aspect of a person's progress—

how they cope with limitations and adjust. This far outweighs the physical side a lot of times. I have guys and ladies who have so much potential to be like a rock star. I know they could go right back to working and having a fulfilling life, but they don't see that. So sometimes, we want more for them than what they want for themselves.

It has a lot to do with how they think about themselves and where they see themselves. Do they see this injury as final? "This is it for me." And Fletcher didn't see it like that. Another factor is that often our younger kids don't fully understand the complexity of their injuries. Sometimes I think that's a benefit for our younger kids—they don't fully understand what all of this means for the future. Many times, the older adults are more jaded, and it's harder for them to have hope and motivation.

The roles are different, too. Younger people don't have all the responsibilities of a husband or wife or working, so they don't stress as much about questions like "What am I going to do now? How am I going to take care of my family? How will I pay my bills?" I think that's a big factor mentally, too.

The biggest source of strength I saw in Fletcher was his faith in God. We had a lot of talks about his faith and why this happened, or if he would ever walk again. He asked me one day, "What if I never walk again?"

I said, "What if you don't?"

"Well," he answered, "I'm going to keep living, as long as God keeps me here."

And I said, "Exactly. You're going to keep living."

When Fletcher faced his challenges, and there were a lot of things that he couldn't do in the beginning. I told him it was going to be hard, but to just keep trying to do them. The more you do the work, the easier it will get for you. He didn't want to go out with his friends in the beginning when he thought about going home, and I said, "No, you have to go hang out with your boys just like you used to before, but you have to teach your boys how to help you."

I think that was one of the biggest things for him, and once he got that, it made a world of difference. I explained that people don't know how to help you unless you tell them how. They want to help you, but they don't know how. So, if you teach them, and you get comfortable teaching people how to help you, you can explain that you can still do some things on your own. To other people, the situation looks overwhelming because they don't understand. You have to tell them, "Oh, I can still go there! But here are some things you can do for me, here's what I need you to look out for, and then we can make this happen."

I explained that other people will start realizing that there really aren't that many limitations; sometimes just a couple more steps are all they have to take to include someone in a wheelchair. As Fletcher got more confident asking for help and explaining his needs, his goals became more realizable because he wasn't going through it alone. He kept getting stronger, and he kept pushing, and every time he accomplished something, he would check it off his list and move on to the next goal. He liked nothing better than to tell his family and friends, "You don't have to help me with that anymore. I can do that myself now."

An example of that was when his dad used to pick him up and transfer him during Fletcher's first few months with us. But Fletcher was transitioning really well toward getting strong enough where he could handle more of that effort himself. So, we would say, "Big Fletch! Quit picking him up— you're going to hurt yourself!"

His dad would always insist, "I'm not gonna hurt myself!" And sure enough, one day, his dad picked him up, and Bam! His back went out. He almost dropped Fletcher, and he was so bent over, he could barely walk himself. We had to go get a wheelchair, put his dad in it, and push him into the hospital next door to be treated for his back.

The Fletcher Cleaves Story

"That's it," we told Fletcher. "Quit letting your dad pick you up—you can do it yourself now." His dad came back later, and he said, "Okay, okay, I guess you guys know what you're talking about." We all laughed because he had been so stubborn about doing this for his boy, promising that nothing was going to happen to his back, and Fletcher was just kind of letting him do it. As soon as his dad stopped picking him up all the time, Fletcher really started making serious progress on his own.

To this day, there are still things we talk about to pursue his next goals. He'll call me up and say, "I really want to work on this, but I don't know how I can do it." And I would show him how to break it into steps and get help on some of the steps until he can do it himself. And that's how he approaches each new challenge—step by step. There are still things that he says he misses doing, of course. But I think he has also found many other things in his life that fulfill him.

When he was getting ready to go home, I told him, "Don't get stuck in this rehab world and miss out on life. You're only going to be 19 or 21 once. Don't miss out on all these things that you want to do, that you wanted to do before, just because you have a spinal cord injury. Keep doing your rehab, but go after your other goals as well."

That's something I really push for when advising the parents. His parents sometimes thought he was giving up on walking if he focused on other goals, such as mastering things with his hands and arms. I explained to the family that these more doable interim goals of independence are important because they enable a person to live life as it is right now. It isn't giving up on the big goals.

We therapists find ourselves becoming very involved with family dynamics in our work, and it can be challenging to find the right words to say to keep moving things forward. My personal relationship with God is a central force in my work. Of course, I realize that everyone has their own take on faith, so the way I handle it is to point out that God is in the miracle-making business whenever someone says things like "I'm never going to walk again." I point out that many people wouldn't have survived the crash they were in or the incident that caused their injury, but they're still here.

I believe there is a reason why that person is still here. I don't know what that reason is, but I know God could have taken them out of here. It's up to each of us to figure out that reason, however we ask or pray. I don't have a crystal ball, so I don't know if any of my patients are ever going to walk again. I pray every morning for all of them that miracles will happen.

I have seen lots of miracles happen. I tell people every day that just walking into the building and being with them humbles me, and it makes me see God every day. When they arrive at the Center and I hear the stories, and when I see pictures of the aftermath of the crashes, it's astounding. These patients are miracles just being here, so who knows what will happen?

I've had quite a few patients who don't even believe in God—period. I've had pastors who said they had become really angry with God and questioned God. All I say is, this is my personal belief, but I'm not trying to push my beliefs on you or anything like that. I'm only answering a question because you asked me a question. If they ask me, "What is the point of my being here when I can't do anything for myself?" I ask them, "Could I tell you my personal belief about it?" If they say yes, then I give my answer, and they take it however they want to take it.

I've had patients who are very angry at everything and everyone, including me, and they don't want anything to do with me. But then a year or two later, they come back to say, "Remember when you talked to me about this?" or "I'm so sorry I was in a really dark place," or "I was really depressed." And I understand. As therapists, we have to pick and choose what to say and when to say it. At the same time, we want to make sure we are being as positive and loving as we can, to make them feel comfortable coming back for more help.

Sometimes, it takes years to build that trusting relationship. I've had patients who, years later, are just getting to the point where they're accepting their injury. Finally, they are ready to start doing things again, like traveling or getting to events, or whatever it is. Some patients are very challenging, and it breaks my heart when I feel that I can't even reach them. Needless to say, I wish everyone had Fletcher's attitude and spirit. It takes a lot of guts to face these challenges.

Fletcher has a never-ending treasure box of little stories in his mind, and we had so many laughs. He would come up with a new joke or some type of story every single day. I asked him, "Do you just make these up or where do you get these from? Because it's insane that you have all of this. I don't know what you are reading or when you have time to come up with this stuff."

He was such a positive patient. He was one of those patients who make you wish you had 12 just like him. He always wanted to make sure you were laughing, instead of waiting for us to make sure he was laughing. He used to love Krispy Kreme donuts. He would actually put a whole donut in his mouth and eat the whole thing. I don't even know how he did it. On his 19th birthday, we ended up getting a dozen donuts for him. We made a donut tower with a little candle on top for his birthday. He went headfirst into it, just eating donuts. We were all incredulous. "Fletcher, you mean you don't want anyone else to have donuts?"

"It's my birthday, it's my cake!" he said. It was hysterical.

It's been about 10 years since he was injured. He still tells me the craziest little stories. He used to call all of us things like PT Ashley—she was the physical therapist he worked with. And then there was OT Leah, and I was TR Shannon. So, we all called him Patient Fletcher. That's still how we refer to each other. He will text me, "TR Shannon, I have a question." And I'll text him back, "What do you want, Patient Fletcher?" He is a nut.

People often wonder where Fletcher gets his unending positive attitude. One place I know Fletcher gets his strength is from his family. They do a lot of stuff together. They regularly go to Chicago for their family reunion. We have an airport outing every month at the Atlanta airport. We take patients through security, we ride the train, we transfer them on and off a plane to practice, and we eat lunch there. Then we come back, so it's like an all-day outing.

When Fletcher told me that they normally would go to Chicago to see family, but they weren't going this time, I told him I was going to get them all to the airport. And he said, "I'm not going to the airport."

His dad agreed. "We're not going."

And I said, "Yeah, you're going, because you said you go every summer to Chicago for the family reunion."

"The next time we get on a plane, Fletcher is going to be walking," his dad said emphatically.

And Fletcher agreed. "Yeah, the next time I get on a plane, I'm not going to need this chair. I'm going to be walking."

"I understand that," I said, "but right now, you're not walking. So, I have to treat you where you're at right now. As you progress, I'll progress with you. If you do the training now and you don't need it in six months to a year, then you can forget everything you just learned about being in the wheelchair. But I feel like this is going to be super beneficial to you because you're going to fly sooner than you know."

Fletcher was pretty stubborn. "No, I'm not wheeling onto a plane. I'm going to be walking."

Finally, I just said, "Fletcher, I need you to trust me. Don't think about anything else—just trust me."

His dad was really reluctant to go through with the training, but Fletcher texted me a year later to say thank you. "Thank you for what?" I asked.

He said, "Thank you for making us go out to the airport for the training session. We're flying to Chicago for our family reunion."

After that, Fletcher had lots and lots of questions about flying and other aspects of traveling in a wheelchair. I would break each task down into steps for him. At first, he was flying throughout the U.S., and then he wanted to go out of the country. I helped him figure out hotels and showering, who was going to travel with him and what they needed to do—all the details.

And now, it's like he can't be stopped. Fletcher has flown an airplane, scuba-dived with whale sharks, ridden on the world's fastest roller coaster, gone parasailing, gone swimming with dolphins during a cruise excursion, and the list goes on. The kid is CRAZY. He is the true definition of living without limitations.

I helped him plan his Vegas trip, and he went jet-skiing a couple years ago. He asked me, "Can I jet-ski?" And I said, "Sure you can," and explained how it could happen safely. It depends on if there's a dock right there. If someone could get the jet ski as close as possible and someone could lower him down, that would work. Or if one person on the jet ski can help him, he can lower himself down. If the jet ski is on the water, and he can get as close as possible to it, then he can back his chair up as close as possible to the jet ski, then two people could help get one leg over, and lift him, or he can hold on and pull himself over. Another option is a sliding board, a board that bridges the gap between his chair and another surface. This allows others to slide him across this board onto the jet ski. Then Fletcher could hold on to the person driving the jet ski.

I've always told Fletcher never to get his mind focused on what he can't do. "Tell me what you want to do, and we will figure it out from there," I would tell him. That's how I approach everything with my patients. It's not their job to figure it out—it's just their job to tell me what they want to do. It's my job to figure out how to make it happen. We worked out so many different things together, and now he hardly needs me for anything. Every once in a while, he'll contact me with a question. He just texted me not too long ago about going on a dune buggy in the Dominican Republic.

When he was still living with his parents in his last year of college, he had landed his job for after graduation. He called with a question. "LaShannon, I want to move out, but I can't cath myself. That's the only thing that's stopping me from being on my own." I told him about a new catheter that had just come out that was designed for quadriplegics. We had some samples in the office, so I took pictures and videos of it for him, and I told him I thought he could do it successfully.

"You really think I can do it?" he asked. For him, it was like a dream come true.

I said, "I definitely know you can do it."

I didn't know that he contacted his vendor and tried it, but when I arrived at his graduation party, his mom informed everyone that I was the therapist from Atlanta who was making it possible for him to move into his own apartment. At first, I was confused, but then Fletcher said, "The catheter! I got it and it's great. I'm out of here!" He was so excited to be on his own, having his friends over, throwing parties and stuff like that. He's very resourceful and does his research, so he is always asking for websites for stuff. He wants to get things solved.

And that's so important for anyone's overall well-being, to have a positive lifestyle and to be ready to ask questions and get help. Fletcher definitely doesn't have any issues asking any type of question—even the very personal questions.

When Fletcher has been scared or unsure of himself, it's always about a girl. He's always thinking about a girl. After he first got home from his therapy, he had a girlfriend and was planning how to go out on dates. He wanted to make sure he didn't feel or look disabled. So, we had a lot of conversations about the things he needed to be able to do for himself if he wanted to have a girlfriend. For instance, she wouldn't want to have to feed him.

In his dating life, he had a lot of heartbreaks, and he would call or text me about it. I told him, "Fletcher, just because you're in a wheelchair, it doesn't exempt you from being heartbroken. That's a part of life. I've been heartbroken plenty of times. If you weren't paralyzed, you'd still get your heart broken."

He said, "I didn't think about it like that." So, those are disappointments that he's overcome as well. He has a better understanding of relationships now that he's older. I have had the honor of watching him grow up. I remember when he was 18. Now he's a mature, grown man.

I think about Fletcher a lot. He's the one patient I don't consider my patient anymore. He will just text me randomly, and it always seems to be at the right moment when I'm facing a difficult patient or some stress in my life. And hearing from him brings me back to being present, to understanding that what I'm going through is not that bad.

Fletcher will send me videos or pictures of something he's doing, and it gives me a new feeling of hope. Seeing his success helps me to keep pushing forward with my current patients because it's going to mean something later on. Maybe not right now, but this is why I do what I do. This is why I love what I do. Fletcher brings that back to me full circle.

So many times, he'll send me a text message or call me, and I'll just say, "Thank you—you made my day." I don't think of him as a patient anymore. I think of him as a friend, even though he's a lot younger than me. He's such a positive person to have in my life. No matter how you're connected to him, you're going to absorb his wonderful attitude.

* * * * * * *

Chapter 8   Don't Tiptoe Through Life

Life is meant to be lived!

At this writing, I'm getting ready to celebrate my 29th birthday and feeling excited about the future. It's crazy how much life has changed in 10 years. I've come so far since my car crash in 2009, and I refuse to give up now. That is why I held a wonderful 10-year commemoration of the crash that changed my life and had a chance to share with loved ones and friends about the amazing journey we have had together.

My therapist from Shepherd Center came down and my teammate from my college football days also came, along with so many friends and family members. You might think a commemoration of such a tragic event would be a solemn time, but it was uplifting, and everyone had a great time. We were all excited to celebrate how far I've come and all that has happened in my life. There was a live band, a raffle, a DJ, food, and drinks, and the event was also the first fundraiser for the launch of my nonprofit, The Sky Is NOT the Limit.

When I started my nonprofit organization, family and friends stepped in to mentor me on things I should look out for, people I should talk to, and how to understand the complexity of running a nonprofit. The Sky Is NOT the Limit strives to inspire, empower, and educate for the betterment of all people. The organization is dedicated to providing support to communities through acts of service, motivational speaking, fundraising campaigns and events, and advocating safe driving.

There's an African proverb that states, "If you want to go fast, go alone. If you want to go far, go together." My support system has definitely helped me come this far. I could not have done any of these things that I have accomplished by myself. It takes a team. For instance, if one of my nurses is late or caught a flat tire or something, or if they decide they don't want to come to work that day, then it makes me late. Whether it's getting ready for a speech, catching a flight, or just going to work, my entire day has been thrown off. It's kind of a domino effect. Relying on other people is something I just deal with and try not to let it get to me.

I try to do as much as I can by myself, and I still fall out of my chair or make a mess trying to do something I've never done before. Not too long ago, in my apartment, I was lying on my bed watching TV, and I thought, 'You know what would be good right now? Chips and salsa!' So I got back into my chair and went to the kitchen. I got the chips off the counter, but for some reason, someone had put the salsa on the shelf above the microwave. I couldn't reach it.

You don't know what you can do until you try, right? So I tried to reach the jar using a ladle, then a wooden spoon, trying to knock the salsa into my lap. I put some towels down on the counter so if the jar hit the counter, it wouldn't break. It was like a game—how can I get this salsa? Finally, the salsa hit the counter and I tried to catch it before it rolled off the counter. Too late. It didn't break, but the top popped off. Most of the salsa ended up on the floor. But I just dipped my chips into what was left in the jar and ate that. So hey, I made a mess, but at least I got my chips and salsa!

I also felt extremely independent when I finally got my truck. Having my truck has been the greatest Godsend of all. I got so tired of relying on people to pick me up and making everyone late because they had to help me. I was never afraid to drive that truck, even from the beginning. I was more excited than anything, and driving it is still my favorite part of the day. I can go wherever I want to go, whenever I want. The only time I need someone is when I'm getting dressed or taking a shower.

If I'm craving some Chipotle or something at night, I just roll up, roll out to my truck, eat, then go home, get undressed, and go to bed. That freedom is what I've been wanting. Being paralyzed, the ultimate goal is to be able to walk again. But in the meantime, being able to do what I want without waiting for other people to sacrifice their time to help me is a wonderful feeling.

I see my parents often, but not as much since I moved out. I live in the heart of downtown Memphis, and they live in the suburbs. I might see them once a week—I'll go over there for Sunday dinner or a weekday evening just to hang out. They're still always helping me, though. If there is something wrong with my chair, my dad will fix it. He'll just pull out his toolbox and fix it. If anything happens, they're always there to help me and make me feel successful.

You might be wondering what happened to Dayne, my roommate who was with me in the car the day of the crash. After the crash, he was badly injured and was in therapy for a semester, and then he went home to Washington, DC, where he went back to college. He played football again in April of the next year. While I was in therapy at Shepherd, we spoke on the phone often and prayed together. He kept track of me, and as we got older, we didn't stay as closely connected since we were living so far apart.

But Dayne has always been and will always be like a brother to me. I tell people that if it weren't for Dayne, I don't know if I would have made it. He saved my life, and he has always been a positive, caring friend. Dayne had angel wings tattooed on his chest with the date of our car crash. Here's what he wrote about our friendship and that fateful day:

By Dayne Mullins

Fletcher and I were inseparable almost immediately. I was glad they put us together as roommates. I clicked with Fletcher instantly, and I knew there was a reason we were put together. And there sure was a reason.

I was an introvert. It was my first college experience, and I didn't want to go out that night. I wanted to sit in our dorm room. Fletcher had to ask me about 30 times to come with him to Buffalo Wild Wings. All I could think about was our first serious scrimmage, and I wasn't about to miss a chance to study up on the playbook and watch my favorite team, the Steelers, play on TV.

But Fletcher kept insisting that we were already the best, and we didn't have to worry about any more preparation. He said going to Buffalo Wild Wings was a good idea for two reasons: There were girls there, and it would be a chance for me to get out. I knew I needed someone to light a fire under me to be more social.

I was always guarding my time and sticking to myself. But Fletcher was adamant that night, and I finally agreed to go. Little did we know that our lives would be forever changed.

After the crash, I struggled with survivor guilt because my injuries were operable, and I was able to go back to the same quality of life as before. I felt so bad about what happened to Fletcher, but with his spirit of perseverance, his faith in God, and the way he was raised, I never had to worry about him hiding away in some kind of nursing home waiting to die.

Even though Fletcher is an amiable, outgoing person, he has the desire to compete against himself and also to be in line with God's plan for him. Fletcher's ability to rise above this challenge is a testament to his spirit and to his ability to always be himself no matter what. He is able to accept himself for who he is, as well as others for who they are, and he continues to strive to be the best version of himself.

On and off the football field, he never stopped working at his personal best. His spirit has never been broken. He has so many gifts and so much patience and courage, and he is a living example of the serenity prayer:

> God, grant me the serenity
> to accept the things I cannot change,
> the courage to change the things I can,
> and the wisdom to know the difference.

Dayne is a friend I can always call up, knowing we'll just pick up where we left off last time, as if no time had passed since we last talked. I am very fortunate to have kept so many good friends who are like brothers and sisters to me. I've known many of them for as long as I can remember.

My longtime friends are with me on many of my trips. I still do plenty of traveling for public speaking. Each speech is different, and each school or organization has people experiencing different things. I never know what I'm going to discover about the people I meet there. That definitely keeps things exciting, and I get lots of questions and especially emails. A lot of people are shy at the speeches, so they just email me afterward to ask me questions.

I had a recent speech at a school earlier this year, and a guidance counselor got in touch with me afterward to let me know how it had affected one of her students. She said, "You won't believe this, but we had this one student we've been trying to reach for the past year and a half. He's been dealing with drugs and comes to school under the influence. He says he doesn't want to go to college, he's been arrested, and he acts like he doesn't have any motivation or interest in taking a better path. He just came to our office and told us your speech made him want to check into rehab. He said he wanted to better himself, and he broke down crying in our office."

I was amazed. I was just telling my story, and I didn't know that could make someone want to check into rehab. I'm glad it happened! Things like this is why I decided to pursue motivational speaking full-time. Other responses I've gotten include things like, "I text and drive, but now I want to stop," or "I've been thinking about what I want to do with my life, and you made me realize that I don't have to give up on myself." Hearing stories like that never gets old.

A lady from Canada emailed me and said she had stage 3 cancer. She was just thinking, 'This is it for me, the Lord is calling me home. My life is over.' Then she saw the short film about me, and she decided to devote herself to fighting the cancer. She told me that because I didn't give up on myself and went on to do all these great things, she didn't want to give up on herself either. She ended up beating cancer, even though she had been literally ready to die prior to seeing the film. I followed up with her a year later, and she said she was doing well; she didn't have cancer anymore. It is so awesome to hear something like this. If my story can help people want to fight for their lives, then I want to keep telling it.

Things continue to move upward. I have my own website now, www.fletchercleaves.com, where I have pictures from speaking engagements, my story, and testimonies from people who have heard me speak. I speak at schools and colleges about how to be safe on the road. I've also spoken at churches about how faith kept my family together through everything. My father always says that before I got hurt, the one thing he wishes was that we had gone to church more often as a family. Once my injury happened, we went there all the time. Church has been a very important part of our healing.

I also speak to a lot of sports teams. Since my injury happened when I was younger, I've made a strong point for people in sports to rely on their education. What would I have done without that? I tell my young audiences how glad I am that I finished high school and took my ACT and SAT tests seriously. If I would have done only the bare minimum, a lot of those state-funded scholarships wouldn't have considered me. That's why I always say, "You never know what's going to happen. When your athletic days end, you need something to fall back on."

Sometimes I speak to kids who are in single-parent homes or foster care. Some may have gone through abuse and other challenges that prevented them from having what most would call a normal childhood. I like to tell them about my situation and how I was always told I was undersized for football, but I ended up getting a scholarship. Also, I tell them how doctors told me I would never do a lot of the things I am doing now, so I encourage them to turn the negatives in their lives into positives.

In my speeches and in my life, I talk a lot about how my family influenced me, how they were always there to pick me up and help me and tell me to always stay positive. If speaking highly to plants helps them grow, imagine if human beings spoke highly to one another all the time. I feel like I'm an example of what can happen when positive affirmation is continuously instilled inside of you. Sometimes I wanted to give up, but my family and friends have always lifted me up and encouraged me to keep working to accomplish things.

I tell people, "Don't let anything stop you. I'm not telling you not to have fun, and I'm not telling you not to live life. What I'm saying is just be safe. I'm all about having fun. My motto is 'Live life to the fullest. Don't tiptoe through life just to arrive safely at death.' Death happens to all of us; it's not something we can run from. You can live life cautiously, but at the end, it turns out the same for all of us, so why not take some chances and follow your dreams?"

My new goal is to travel solo. I'm still at a point in my life that I rely on someone traveling with me for safety purposes, especially if I'm on a plane. If I'm flying somewhere, I need at least one person with me. It would be nice to be able to fly by myself. I'd love to be able to just check into a hotel and deal with travel delays on my own, but I'm not that independent yet.

Even though my life still involves relying on someone else one way or the other at certain times of the day, I keep setting goals for myself of greater and greater independence. Of course, I haven't given up on walking on my own, and I never will.

In my speeches, I tell the audience, "Although you might not be in an ideal situation right now, you have the power to change that. You make your own decisions. Life is all about choices. Whatever you're going through right now won't last forever. I've never seen a cloud hang over one person's house for long. The storm that you're going through will eventually pass. Don't let your environment or your circumstances dictate your future. The sky is NOT the limit. There are NO limits in life!"

* * * * * * *

Acknowledgments

I'd like to thank those who helped me construct this book: Sedrik Newbern, my publisher; Linda Wolf and Sade Baker, my editors; LaShannon Ali, my therapist from Shepherd Center; and Dayne Mullins, my college roommate and friend.

I'd also like to thank my entire therapy team from Shepherd Center, my family, friends, support system, and especially "The Crew" for helping me live this crazy life.

Last but not least, I want to thank you for reading this book. The sky is NOT the limit!

Have to learn to barbecue before
I leave for college!

First day at the dorm with Dayne.

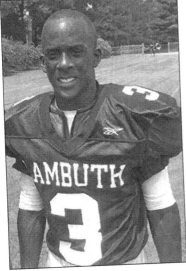
First collegiate scrimmage.

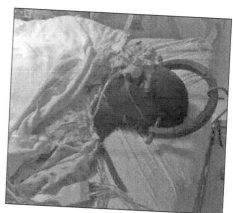
Hours after the crash with
the halo on my head.

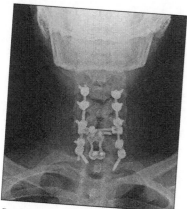
Rods in my neck after surgery.

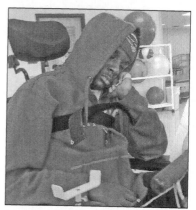
Eight-hour therapy days are no joke. Tired!

College teammates waiting to see me at the hospital.

The infamous donut cake.

My Shepherd Center therapy team.

Never a dull moment with my frat brothers.

Radio interview in New York, New York. So nice, they named it twice.

A dream come true, being on SportsCenter.

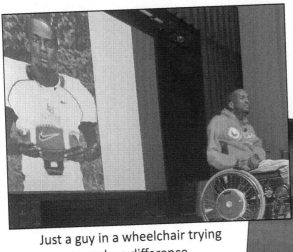

Just a guy in a wheelchair trying to make a difference.

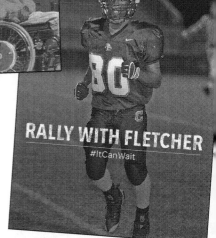

AT&T "It Can Wait" poster (last high school game).

Does anybody have any questions?

Showing off my new logo during a speech.

Safe Driving presentation at AutoZone headquarters.

Thankful for friends who won't leave me behind.

Riding a dolphin in Mexico.

Beautiful weather and beautiful ladies
in Barbados.

Jet skis in Barbados.
("Don't lean, brutha.")

Get your monkey off me, Bro! (Dominican Republic)

Friends helping me swim in the Dominican Republic.

Look, Ma! No hands!

When in Rome, do as the Romans do.

Crazy how just a few years
prior, I was in the ICU.

"Love my brothers, cut them in
on anything."—Drake

Splashin' in high fashion
in Dubai.

World's tallest building,
Burj Khalifa in Dubai.

Burj Al Arab, the world's only
7-star hotel.

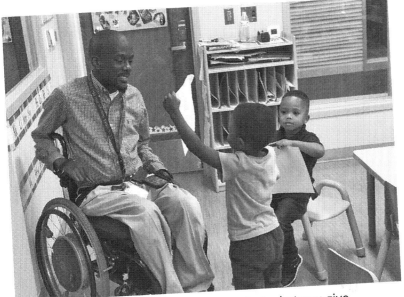

Life is not about what you have, but what you give.

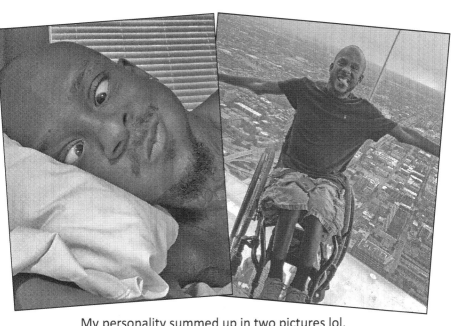

My personality summed up in two pictures lol.
(Chicago)

"I alone cannot change the world, but I can cast a stone across the water to create many ripples."
—Mother Teresa

Mother, father, grandmother— the reasons behind it all!

The Sky Is NOT the Limit nonprofit donating supplies.